THE COMPLETE CARTOONS OF
THE
NEW YORKER

THE COMPLETE CARTOONS OF
THE
NEW YORKER

EDITED BY ROBERT MANKOFF

FOREWORD BY DAVID REMNICK

INTRODUCTION TO THE PAPERBACK EDITION BY ADAM GOPNIK

BLACK DOG
& LEVENTHAL
PUBLISHERS
NEW YORK

ACKNOWLEDGMENTS

So many people have contributed to this project in the two years it took to create it that to credit all of them properly would take a book in itself, or perhaps even a DVD. A fascinating idea, but perhaps not commercially viable.

A giant book/electronic anthology like this demands the talents and skills of many dedicated people. Fortunately for me, such people were available at *The New Yorker*, the Cartoon Bank, and Black Dog & Leventhal Publishers. Their efforts were invaluable in refining and developing ideas for the anthology and implementing them digitally and on paper.

Black Dog & Leventhal was an integral part of the project from the beginning. Its president, J. P. Leventhal, stuck with the project when difficulties seemed insuperable and committed the resources and personnel necessary to make them superable. The book's editor, Laura Ross, was tireless but never tiresome in her efforts to keep everyone on task. Matt Dellinger, at *The New Yorker*, along with Cory Whittier, Sumner Jaretzki, and Jay Sciarra at the Cartoon Bank, were her partners in vigilance. Marshall Hopkins was invaluable in many ways, and merely valuable in others.

It required extraordinary graphic sensibilities to bring this huge book to life with its own voice. And Toshiya Masuda, True Sims, Greg Captain, Shana Davis, Owen Phillips, and Kilian Schalk did that and more,

making it sing as well. Steven Louie translated the song, appropriately enough, onto a DVD.

Because this book draws on the rich history of *The New Yorker*, the magazine's staff had much to offer, and generously did so. Ben Greenman served as assistant editor of the book and as a general sounding board; he also wrote the thematic essays throughout. Lee Lorenz, who was for many years the magazine's art editor, furnished institutional memory, guidance, and perspective. His firsthand knowledge of the cartoonists of *The New Yorker* made him an ideal choice to write the biographical profiles that appear here.

I also want to thank David Remnick, Pamela McCarthy, and the other editors for their support, suggestions, and close reading of all the material. David and Pam, more than anyone else, are responsible for gathering and integrating the considerable literary talents on display. And those talents have my enduring, penultimate thanks.

Ultimate thanks go to the cartoonists of *The New Yorker*, past and present, every last one of them, for helping us to see the sublime in the ridiculous, and for reminding me every day why I have the best job in the world.

Robert Mankoff
Cartoon Editor

First paperback edition published in 2006.

For licensing inquiries, or to purchase prints of cartoons, please contact The Cartoon Bank, a division of The New Yorker Magazine, 28 Wells Ave., Bldg. 3, Yonkers, NY 10701;
ph: 1-800-897-8666; international calls: 1-914-478-5527
e-mail: toon@cartoonbank.com

ISBN-10: 1-57912-620-0
ISBN-13: 978-1-57912-620-9

The Library of Congress has cataloged the hardcover as follows:

The complete cartoons of the New Yorker / edited by Robert Mankoff; foreword by David Remnick.
p. cm.
Includes index.
ISBN 1-57912-322-8
1. Caricatures and cartoons   United States. 2. American wit and humor, Pictorial.
3. New Yorker (New York, N.Y. : 1925) I. Mankoff, Robert. II. New Yorker (New York, N.Y. : 1925)

NC1428.N47C66 2004
741.5'973   dc22
2004046371

Book design: Toshiya Masuda

Manufactured in China

Published by
Black Dog & Leventhal Publishers, Inc.
151 West 19th Street
New York, New York 10011

Distributed by
Workman Publishing Company
708 Broadway
New York, New York 10003

b d f h j i g e c a

CONTENTS

EDITOR'S NOTE

ROBERT MANKOFF

Y ou have in your hands "The Complete Cartoons of The New Yorker," every cartoon ever published in *The New Yorker*— I hope. I really do, because we've tried very hard to be totally inclusive. From the start of the process, we were relentless, unsparing, obsessive, compulsive, and even possessed in our efforts. We examined every single page of *The New Yorker* published since 1925 to ensure that not a single cartoon was missed. In the end, after examining more than four hundred thousand pages, we found *70,363* cartoons. That's one for each resident of Springfield, Ohio, according to the 2000 census, with enough left over for quite a few pets.

Still, I'm haunted by the possibility that we missed one. And, much as I hate to admit it, it is a possibility. So there's ten bucks for anyone who can find any cartoon that we missed. We're quite

"Wake up you mutt!
We're getting married today."

serious about this, or, as befits the genre we're celebrating, semi-serious. If you know of any cartoon that appeared in *The New Yorker* and that we have omitted, please tell us about it.

But, please, don't tell us about the Peter Arno cartoon at the left.

I'm being proactive here, because a lot of people, myself included, are convinced that it's a *New Yorker* cartoon. It's a great cartoon, and it has all the hallmarks of cartoon humor that *The New Yorker* was pioneering at the time—a single-line caption and a carefully thought-out, integrated situation in which image and caption are interdependent. Now, why Harold Ross, the magazine's editor, chose not to publish it I don't know, but it never appeared in the magazine or in any *New Yorker* cartoon album. Until now, that is.

No, the sad truth is that not every great cartoon published in the last eighty-two years appeared in *The New Yorker*. It just

seems that way. There's also this Shel Silverstein classic, which people often ask about. Well, I wish we had published it, but Shel was a great cartoonist for *Playboy* who never appeared in *The New Yorker*, and this particular cartoon wasn't even published in *Playboy*, but appeared in *Look,* in 1956. So we're going to make do with the 70,363 that we did publish.

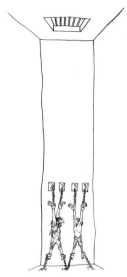

"Now, here's my plan . . ."

Before we did all that collecting and counting and checking, we thought we would publish a book with *all* the cartoons in it. We nixed that idea when our math department crunched the numbers: $70,363/3=23,454$, where 23,454 is the number of pages in the book if there is an average of three cartoons on a page. A book with pages the size of barn doors was deemed impractical. And the idea of printing postage-stamp-size cartoons and viewing them through a magnifying glass, in the manner of the compact Oxford English Dictionary, appealed only to lexicographers / philatelists.

But where paper folded under pressure, a DVD spun in to save the day. Using the latest advances in nanotechnology, teeny-weeny shoehorns were used to jam all the cartoons in the magazine's history, from February 21, 1925, until February 23, 2006, onto one DVD-ROM. Then, using fairly old advances in glueology, that disk was stuck to the inside front cover of the book.

One could say that the DVD was the director's cut of the book if the director hadn't cut out anything at all. Here you can find every cartoon on topics as diverse as:

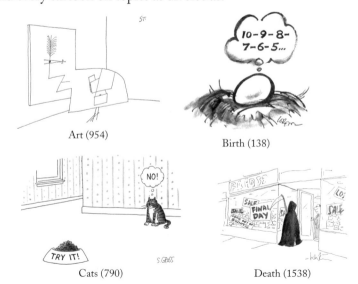

Art (954)

Birth (138)

Cats (790)

Death (1538)

Education (1068)

France (262)

Golf (363)

Humpty-Dumpty (13)

Internet (98)

Judges (667)

Khrushchev (22)

Lions (244)

Money (6560)

Nixon (132)

Obesity (81)

Politics (2921)

Queens (143)

Religion (1422)

Sex (2686)

Technology (1401)

Urban Life (1519)

Vacations (2014)

Witches (182)

X-rays (26)

The Yankees (29)

Zoos (215)

Did I leave anything out?

Only about forty thousand cartoons, but now you know where to find them.

Or perhaps you'd like to leave the disk in its case for a while, and spend some time with the big, big book you are holding. The book, big, big as it is, has much less than the disk and, at the same time, much more. It has more beauty, for starters: pixels and computer screens can't do justice to the lush washes of an Arno or an Addams, the delicate charcoals of a Robert Weber or a Charles Saxon, or the eloquent line of a Saul Steinberg. In the book the cartoons can be reproduced full size, as they originally appeared in the magazine, and even, in some cases, oversized. Also, they're on paper, and what was created with ink on paper looks best re-created with ink on paper.

The book involved, necessarily, a great deal more editorial decision-making. After all, we had to select from the 70,363 (there's that number again) the 2,083 that could be included in the book. We wanted the cartoons for each year, and each decade, to be a comic snapshot, a funhouse mirror, of their time. By picking the cartoons that were most representative of the modes of thought, the desires, and the conventions that spawned them, we'd be offering a history of *The New Yorker* cartoon and a bit of cultural history rolled into one. We've also supplied a written guide to each era by some of the sharpest chroniclers of culture to appear in *The New Yorker*. The reflections of *New Yorker* writers were a special treat for me. I'm a big fan of theirs. I often wonder where they get *their* ideas. And, unlike most people, I read the articles first.

FOREWORD

DAVID REMNICK

From the earliest days of *The New Yorker*, the magazine's founder and first editor, Harold Ross, presided over an art meeting every Tuesday afternoon. The main work at hand was to sort through hundreds of "roughs," or sketches, that were being proposed as cartoons for the magazine. Although the final decisions were Ross's to make, he invited a rotating cast of editors and assorted kibbitzers to the meeting. (It's a practical impulse. Laughing alone is not easy. Try it.) During those sessions, which often went on for four or five hours, Ross did not merely go through the stack of roughs pronouncing "yea" or "nay." With his assistant, Miss Terry, at his side, he dictated countless suggestions about the drawings, and no detail was considered beneath comment and reconsideration: *Take this down, Miss Terry. . . . There never was a sky like that. . . . Which elephant is talking? . . . That isn't a butler—it's a banker!* At one such meeting in 1933, Ross came to a drawing by Carl Rose with the caption "Speak, Mr. Pennywhistle, speak to me." Thanks to the archives, we have his note to Rose as dictated to Miss Terry: "Reduce Mr. Pennywhistle and make him concave." Peter De Vries, a *New Yorker* writer who had a stint as an art-meeting adjutant, recalled to James Thurber how Ross once lingered in silence for a full two minutes over a drawing of a Model T automobile making its way down a dusty country road. "Take this down, Miss Terry," he said at last. "Better dust."

Thurber, who began attending art meetings long before he began submitting drawings of his own, wrote of Ross that he was "by far the most painstaking, meticulous, hairsplitting, detail-criticizer the world of editing has known." *The New Yorker* was Ross's creation, the result of both his Jazz Age inspiration and the many years of labor and reinventions that followed, and Thurber, De Vries, and the rest told their Ross stories always out of a sense of gratitude and affection. Well, almost always. The writer Ben Yagoda spent years in the archives researching his history of the magazine, and among the things he unearthed is a record of the artists' occasional fury at Ross's meddling. In 1937, for example, William Steig, one of the real masters of the form, wrote in despair to another art-meeting attendee, William Maxwell, "Once again I am completely flabbergasted by the editorial decisions. Out of a group of drawings expounding a particular idea one is chosen with the recommendation that the situation be reversed. . . . Frankly I don't want any collaborators. Would you? Would you like someone to suggest that you select a paragraph from one of your stories, change it so that it becomes the opposite of what you intended, and throw away the rest? I appeal to you as a fellow human-being. Is the whole world going mad?"

Poor Maxwell. One day he was being appealed to by Steig as a "fellow human-being"—take note that the artist did not address the editor himself on such a basis—and then he found himself writing to another artist, Chon Day, at Ross's instruction. "One of your roughs—the one about the father breaking the unbreakable doll—seemed to us a possible idea," Maxwell informed Day, "but Mr. Ross is troubled by the fact that a man wouldn't use a sledge hammer in the house, and thinks the scene had better be in the back yard with the doll placed on a large stone, or on the floor of the garage. Also he thinks it would be better if the mother were distressed and the child were in tears." One imagines that Chon Day was soon in tears. One imagines further that when Day was sufficiently recovered from his weeping he constructed an effigy of Ross and swiftly reduced it to bits—with the swing of an indoor-operating sledgehammer.

As an editor, I don't know what to say about reforming this painful artist-editor relationship other than to proffer a kind of eternal apology and then continue to ask questions about making Mr. Pennywhistle concave. We have, it is true, moved the art meetings from Tuesday to Wednesday, but I readily admit that this is a minor, perhaps meaningless reform.

What has certainly not changed is that the cartoons are essential to *The New Yorker*. They are what readers read first. (Don't lie. You know it's true.) They set the tone of the magazine. They are, in fact, the emblem of the magazine and, as far as I can tell, the longest-running popular comic genre in American life. ("The Simpsons" has been around for fifteen years, "Saturday Night Live" for thirty, *New Yorker* cartoons for eighty.) The longer one is charged with selecting cartoons for the magazine, the clearer it becomes how miraculous they are, how difficult to devise and draw. The best cartoons are exquisite explosive devices. When they are constructed just so, they produce an explosion (our laughter), but when they are not, they don't. It is also remarkable how closely readers pay attention to the subtleties, the evolving genres, the mix of topical jokes and social criticism. Not long ago, a young woman approached me and said she was writing her doctoral dissertation on the changes that have taken place in the genre of the talking-dog cartoon.

This book, and the disk enclosed with it, does something we have never tried before. On paper and electronically, you have in your hands every cartoon we have ever published. And yet, somehow, it's not quite enough. I apologize to you, dear Reader, and, above all, to the artists, for I am sure—I am absolutely positive—that every week in the art meeting we reject at least some roughs that, at least for some readers, would have made fantastic, combustible cartoons. Editorial judgment is subjective. To hear James Thurber on the subject, editorial judgment is worse than that. Here, in a letter written in 1937, Thurber is thoroughly exasperated, and he announces that he is resubmitting a drawing that Ross rejected, and he is asking for—no, *demanding*—reconsideration and acceptance: "If this drawing is not funny, and is not a swell drawing, I shall engage to eat it, and with it all of Price's fantasies that just miss, all of Taylor's S. Klein women, and all eleven versions of every drawing Day does of two men in a restaurant. I will also eat every drawing of a man and a woman on a raft, every drawing of a man and a native woman on a desert island, and every drawing of two thin women in big-backed chairs. . . . I will also eat every drawing of a small animal talking to its parents, and every drawing of two large animals talking about their young."

The archives do not record which of Thurber's drawings he was resubmitting or whether Ross reconsidered. Perhaps you will find it here, one delight among sixty-odd thousand others.

ART CONFERENCE

THE FUNNY PICTURE IS REJECTED BECAUSE YOU CAN'T TELL WHO IS TALKING, THE OLD LADY OR THE FIREMAN, AND BECAUSE WE HAD A PICTURE OF A MAN TRYING TO GET A DRINK AT A DAM. BESIDES, HOW DID THE OLD LADY GET THROUGH THE POLICE LINES?

INTRODUCTION TO THE PAPERBACK EDITION
ADAM GOPNIK

The world is filled with funny drawings. Cartoon and caricature, though not as old as people sometimes think, have been, since at least the seventeenth century, a common language of popular entertainment. Every age and nation has its favorite funny drawings and has—or used to have, anyway—magazines to contain them. And because the world *is* filled with funny drawings and old magazines, a small but worthwhile question arises: why these drawings, why this magazine? What makes this sight different from all other sights? What makes a *New Yorker* cartoon as instantly recognizable and as different from a cartoon in the old *Punch* as it is from a cartoon in the old *Playboy* (where many cartoons too racy for *The New Yorker* used to emigrate, looking lost but happy)?

The first thing we might do is emancipate the drawings in this book, which date from the birth of the magazine, in the fizzy twenties, to its current hard breathing in the anxious aughts, from being too neatly tied to social history, too neatly keyed to the preoccupations of the time. Of the many memories that *New Yorker* cartoons bring to mind, few are narrowly topical. It is obvious that cartoons from the thirties will show people in a Depression and those from the sixties will show men on or on their way to the moon. But these are the small change of the time, and thousands of editorial cartoons show that history just as well. When we think of the *New Yorker* cartoon we don't remember particular "issues" or even (terrible admission) particular gags or captions.

Of course, some captions have been permanently engraved in our minds, from "I say it's spinach, and I say the hell with it" to "How about never—is never good for you?" and "On the Internet, nobody knows you're a dog." But we don't pause at night and recall gags; we shut our eyes and see pictures. When we think of the *New Yorker* cartoon we think first of all of pictured people, social types made visible.

Rarely topical in the narrow editorial sense, the *New Yorker* cartoon has always been typical—a registry of social characters as they occur in the world. Some of these are already part of Americana: Helen Hokinson's stately, alarmed matrons; Peter Arno's angular revelers; James Thurber's bald, baleful husbands and looming Connecticut Amazons; Edward Koren's scratchy, happy mothers with their vast down coats and earnest therapeutic-minded optimism; Roz Chast's slope-shouldered, high-pantsed, hopelessly post-modern misfits. But we are also haunted by types drawn by those cartoonists who are more cult than brand name: James Stevenson's Park

Avenue-and-Southampton complacents; Lee Lorenz's lecherous admen, ties wide and eyes alight; Chon Day's worried corporate managers with their anxious diagonal eyebrows; Barney Tobey's wise children. And then there are cartoonists who can make social types out of architecture itself, as with Frank Modell's beautifully spare black-and-white museums or Charles Saxon's sober views of International Style buildings. And sometimes it is simply the atmosphere in which the characters move that we remember: Whitney Darrow, Jr.'s wonderful chiaroscuro creating a shadowy, Cheever-like world of dark apartments and bright hopes; or Robert Mankoff's stipple, its vanishing softness so delicately at odds with his hard-edged jokes.

Each one of these cartoonists does something more than make us laugh—or, if there is nothing *more* than that, something *other* than make us laugh. They sum up whole states of mind and particular moments in the history of manners through a few small pencil marks. It is the ability of the *New Yorker* cartoonists—enwrapped, if not entombed, within these pages—to inventory our reality without exhausting our attention. They're able, in a way terrifying to a writer who needs two thousand words in the middle of the magazine to do something even remotely similar, to capture the specifics of a period, a style, a moment in time, with a few scrawls and washes. We ham-handed non-drawers can only look on with wonder at these often unsung and probably underpaid (as they will be the first to tell you) stenographers of the human condition as it occurred in and around Manhattan Island over the last century.

The *New Yorker* cartoon style, though far from uniform, is distinct among the world's cartooning styles because, for all its ellipses and simplifications, it always carries within it a small seed of realism, and gets its effects more by being truthful than by being wild, more by being right than by being wacky. Harold Ross's famous impatience about the "itness" of the cartoons submitted to him every week—"That isn't a butler, it's a banker," "Is the woman on the bookcase alive, or stuffed, or just dead?"—which has been carried on by his successors, is not merely persnickety. Ross intuitively recognized that a good cartoon ought to be a little window on the world.

For a long time, those who drew and edited *New Yorker* cartoons called them "drawings," and, though that bit of idiom is no longer as absolute as it once was, it carried within it a clue about what makes them special. They are drawings first, gags second. The *New Yorker* cartoon has been, on the whole, vivid but not broad. Where the comic strip and cartoon have a close relation to the grotesque and the grimacing, the *New Yorker* cartoon, emerging happily from British and American illustration, has been a lighter and, on the whole, calmer form of realism. The *New Yorker* cartoon was one of the bright side alleys, and has become one of the few remaining outposts, of the twenties and thirties styles of American lyric-realist illustration. The great majority of *New Yorker* cartoonists have never been plain outline and cookie-cutter contour men and women, but earnest pen-and-ink-wash artisans trying to embody a three-dimensional world. There is a close relation between the manner of the *New Yorker* cartoonists of the twenties and thirties and the painters of that Silver Age of American realism, and it is the art of the realist painters of that time—Pène du Bois and Stettheimer, and Marsh—whose miniaturized manner of delight, that faux-naif relish of Central Park and Fifth Avenue and the people who inhabit them, rings and resonates sympathetically in the *New Yorker* pages. (In fact, the sententious author was about to write about the close relation of a typical *New Yorker* cartoon of the thirties with Reginald Marsh's etchings when he discovered that the cartoon he had in mind to praise for its precocity was, in fact, by Reginald Marsh. You can see it on page seventy-two.) When the great and final reckoning of American style is made it will be our realisms that count, and the *New Yorker* drawing will have played its part in their making, much as the cartoons and drawings of Daumier and Guys played theirs in the making of French urban realism in the nineteenth century.

But that observational and realist urge has also always been in tension with an American impatience, expressed in moments of extreme simplification. Looking at the work of Peter Arno, the first indisputable genius of the *New Yorker* cartoon, one is knocked out by how many abbreviations and telegraphic simplifications he invented that have endured: the Xs that replace his clubmen's eyes and indicate drunkenness and the Os with which his chorines stare out with dewy-dumb eroticism are by themselves magical stenography. These self-conscious stylizations, that Deco Egyptian chrome feeling of Covarrubias and Soglow, evoke the streamlined twenties, and they are richly represented in this book. But, though present, they are not, on the whole, the mainstream of the *New Yorker* cartoon; they lightened the load without altering it.

It is through the tension between the need to simplify, to set the idea down quick in a few recognizable hieroglyphs, and the desire to get it right, to show the surface of manners as they are, that the best *New Yorker* cartoons are made. The play between these two desires—to make a joke visible and to make it visible as something other than a joke—is what gives these pages their life and energy. It is in the push and pull between comic simplification and social reporting that the real genius of the *New Yorker* drawing lies. Together, the urge to get a lit- tle piece of reality right and the urge to make something funny drain mockery of its easy malice, its cheaply generalizing point-scoring, its pseudo-satirical obviousness.

This makes the classic *New Yorker* cartoon something genuinely new in the world: a style of satirical serenity. It is satire without over-exaggeration, satire that chooses to represent itself as reporting, satire without taking sides—mockery without moralizing. This implicit serenity, this charmed neutrality, is bound to be annoying to those who prefer more obvious styles of indignation, but it accounts for the extraordinarily happy effect the *New Yorker* cartoon has on its readers, for the constant reiteration of the magazine's addicts that they turn first to the cartoons. They love them because they are funny, but they love them even more because they are sane. There have been dull *New Yorker* cartoons, but there has never been a tendentious one. (Viewed from within the magazine, a cartoon's sanity lightens the column of type that adjoins it; to be on the same page with something narrowly witty, modestly funny, makes the writer feel that he is these things, too. Wit is not contagious, but elegance of mind creates an illusion of continuity, infecting the whole page.)

Of course, no formula or analysis can account for an artist, much less for that handful of unaccountable geniuses who live within these pages but somehow manage to float above them in the annoying way that genius does. They include the great Thurber, who, for effort, hardly ought to be counted as an artist at all, but who drew the "neuter outline that's the plan/And icon of the Industrial Man," as Auden wrote. The work of Charles Addams, even after decades of exploitation and commercial cheapening, still seems magical and unrivalled in its absolute determination to record the world as it is and to make it strange, too. And Saul Steinberg, the Picasso of the printed page, never ceased being a cartoonist, though it was a word he loathed. (He loathed the word for the same reason he loathed being called Romanian, or Jewish, or bald, though he was all of these things, too: a genius is a spy, passing through other people's categories and borders, and hates having his passport stamped, even correctly.)

The *New Yorker* cartoon at its best has continued to take on some of the tasks of fiction after fiction has largely given them up: to mummify manners, to fix the traits and tics of urban life, to show the way we live. In the end, this ability to register the changing surface of the world without ever retreating into mere illustration, to make a plurality of worlds through a plurality of styles, is what makes us return again and again to these drawings, long after their ostensible subjects have passed into memory. The *New Yorker* cartoon is an unpretentious form, meant to give nothing but pleasure, but, turning these pages, one wonders if each of these artists does not in fact give us, with a lovely modesty, just what we want from all art, large and small, high and low, funny and sober: the light of a time passed through the prism of a mind.

INDUSTRIAL CRISES

The day a cake of soap sank at Procter & Gamble's

THE FIRST DECADE
1925-1934

THE FIRST DECADE
1925-1934

ROGER ANGELL

In October, 1925, eight months after *The New Yorker's* first issue appeared, its founding editor, Harold Ross, complained, "Everybody talks of *The New Yorker's* art, that is, its illustrations, and it has been described as the best magazine in the world for a person who can not read." A brilliant if irritable intuiter, Ross got this exactly right, as I can attest. My mother, Katharine Angell, later Katharine White, had joined the magazine's staff in its first weeks, and the galleys and drawings and rough copies she brought home at night soon became vivid primers and lesson books for five-year-old me. I was reading by six, and if I couldn't make much of the captions at first, there was plenty of dialogue-free art to feed on: Al Frueh's running series "Solving the Traffic Problem," for instance, which proposed triangular automobiles, or parking lots on apartment-house balconies; or Ralph Barton's terrifying ashman heaving his empty cans about at six in the morning. I read the newspaper funnies, of course, but also ate up the magazine's strip drawings—like Frueh's journey of a much handled restaurant bun, from a squalid basement bakery through sooty streets and along to a diner's pristine butter plate. I didn't understand Rea Irvin's "The Rise and Fall of Man"—four profiled heads, from primate to Neanderthal, Socrates to William Jennings Bryan—but worked at it. Kids dig art, and I can almost recapture the first thrill of Peter Arno's roadster driver hanging a left in front of a hurtling locomotive, and my riveted interest in Gardner Rea's wiggly ink line, which could encompass a sunset and full seaside, under an endless sky. I was just entering second grade when Gluyas Williams's "Industrial Crises" series presented a sinking moment at Procter & Gamble, and once somebody reminded me that these were the people who made Ivory soap I got the joke, because their "It Floats" motto came with every bar. Then I went back for a long second look at the P. & G. board member flinging off his clothes, and the heroic deep-sea diver, and the twenty or thirty astounded faces at the Natatorium door. Goodbye, Christopher Robin!

The grand theme I shared with the magazine's first artists was New York itself, the soaring and subterranean creature that was coming to life around us day by day. Like other city kids my age, I sucked up the sounds and sights of the Chrysler Building, the Empire State, the George Washington Bridge, the East

River Drive, and the new IND subway system as they were being built. Late one night, my father woke me up and rushed me and my sister downtown to watch a spectacular fire on the topmost levels of the half-finished Sherry Netherland skyscraper. All this stir and change showed up in the magazine, of course. An I. Klein pedestrian falling into a hole in the ground asks a pick-wielder, "Is this the I.R.T. or the B.M.T.?" Alan Dunn's construction worker sends up a Swiss-on-rye sandwich by crane-lift, and Leonard Dove's riveter, clinging upside down to a scary high beam, murmurs that beer at lunch always makes him drowsy. (Looking over this stuff now, you can almost sense some of the magazine's less accomplished artists beginning to falter because they couldn't handle perspective.) Garrett Price, looking up instead of down, fills his page with a tangle of overhead beams and cranes and catwalks, to set up the yawning worker in the foreground, who drops his hammer by his feet and sighs, "Oh, the hell with it."

There has never been a younger or livelier assemblage of artists than the group that found its way onto the magazine's pages in the late twenties and came back again the next week and the week after that: Otto Soglow, Barbara Shermund, Peter Arno, Helen Hokinson, Alan Dunn, Perry Barlow, Carl Rose, Mary Petty, and, in 1930, James Thurber. Many of them were still getting their act together, but, as the former art editor Lee Lorenz has observed, Hokinson arrived fully formed. Her over-dressed suburban matrons and club ladies were foolish but gallant, and encouraged *New Yorker* subscribers, a middle-class and increasingly suburban bunch, to laugh at themselves a little, even as they felt the sophisticate's kick of superiority. Her two hatted museumgoers circling a Brancusi shape, with explanatory leaflets in hand, are clearly us.

Arno's array of lipsticked nymphs, narrow young men in top hats and tuxedos, and ogling old gents (like the one lifting a brassiere from a street-sweeper's gatherings) were stamped on the page with such brio that he almost convinced America that everybody in New York stayed up every night, drank too much, and had too much fun. When my parents went out in their evening clothes, my mother in a glittering Lanvin top, I thought they were off to join Arno's gang. Maybe they had the same wish.

*"Hey, Ed! They didn't have no baloney
so I got Swiss on rye."*

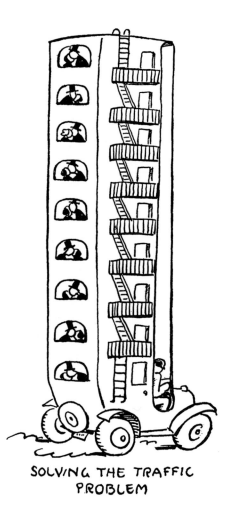

SOLVING THE TRAFFIC
PROBLEM

THE 1930'S
Weekend Guests—Sunday Morning after Saturday Night

Arno, a Yale guy with slicked-down hair, a twenties jaw, and bright teeth, was married to Lois Long, the magazine's fashion writer: the first and only *New Yorker* glam couple. He depended on editors and idea men for many of his cartoons, but there was a powerful fall of light and shadow in everything he did, including his breathtaking covers. He kept at it for forty-three years, with unfading zing, and perhaps still ranks as the magazine's primo artist.

Sex and speakeasies, kept bimbos, shiny long cars, servants, and terrible hangovers—look at Ralph Barton's "Weekend Guests—Sunday Morning After Saturday Night"—implied a world of moneyed privilege, as did Rea Irvin's Eustace Tilley on the first cover; one can wonder whether Ross hadn't been yearning for someone like the Bronx-born William Steig to turn up, as he did in 1930, and balance the social scales. Steig, at twenty-two, knew about families in their underwear and kids playing street games, but Ross, in truth, loved him because he was funny. The magazine uneasily found room for the market crash of '29 but generally passed up breadlines and economic despair because there was no way to do them lightly. One exception was William Crawford Galbraith's opulent babe reclining near her bald sugar daddy, who tells a friend, "I never told her about the Depression. She would have worried." In any case, artists like Thurber and George Price inhabited worlds of their own. Looking at Thurber's seal camped at the head of that bed, or his decapitating "Touché!" fencer, I wondered how anyone who couldn't draw could dare draw so well. Thurber was a friend of my new stepfather, E. B. White, who first persuaded Ross that Thurber's idle scrawlings were great art. In 1934, Jim gave me the original of his mysterious "What have you done with Dr. Millmoss?," which was foully filched from my Third Form dormitory room at Pomfret School. (Interpol has promised an arrest in this case any day now.)

By the end of 1934, *The New Yorker* had a circulation of a hundred and twenty-four thousand, and its big pre-Christmas issue (which included the celebrated John O'Hara story "Over the River and Through the Wood") ran to a hundred and forty-four pages. The Thurber drawing that week had a drunk looking over a lunchtime restaurant stuffed with women and snarling

"You gah dam pussy cats!" The magazine's cartoon art had done away with long captions and explained jokes, and could look forward to the exploration of its bright new format by talents like Robert Day, whose Hoover Dam in the October 13th issue was filling up with water on the wrong side of the wall, and Richard Decker, who (in the issue of December 1st) came up with a lavishly rendered desert island, of all things. "Perhaps we ought to set up some simple form of government," one castaway proposes to the other. The future was uncertain but would probably turn out O.K. Charles Addams's maiden drawing, in the issue of February 4, 1933, depicted a National Hockey League player who'd forgotten his skates. Saul Steinberg, as yet unknown, was living in Italy but thinking of making a change; George Booth was six, Ed Koren two years shy of his birth, and Roz Chast a couple of decades away from a first look at her unkempt world.

At lunch one day earlier that same year, at my mother and stepfather's place in Maine, I remarked that I probably knew the subject and caption of every cartoon *The New Yorker* had ever published. "It's not possible," White said. "There must be thousands by now." But when he got down some of the bound volumes from their shelf and put me through a little quiz it turned out that I was right. I can't remember what any of us made of this goofy feat, but I hope I told myself that I was a kid who'd appreciated his privileges.

"Pardon me. Is this the I.R.T. or the B.M.T.?"

"It's broccoli, dear."
"I say it's spinach, and I say the hell with it."

"Er—you didn't come across a perfectly ah—ravishing lipstick down there, did you?"

Drawn by Hanley.

"Pa, what's all this talk about Evolution?"
"Son, I'll have to consult my attorney before I can answer
that question. I might be sent to jail for it."

Wife: "I'm not angry, I'm only terribly hurt!"

"You may pull the plug, now, Nurse. I have finished."

THE TOMATO SURPRISE

1925

Club Attendant (Aghast): "M'Gawd.
Bill, that one MOVED!"

Uncle: Poor girls, so few get their wages!
Flapper: So few get their sin, darn it!

"I don't know what I shall do, Amelia,
when I think of you alone in Paris."

"Where to?"
"None of your damn business."

"What's the dog waiting for?"
"Oh, nothing . . . once in a while I cut a piece
off the ear—she just loves that."

Proposed Bootleggers' Wing at the Metropolitan

1926

"Who was that gentleman I seen you with last night?"
"That was no gentleman, that was my wife."

"Cheer up, dearie, here come the balloons."

Solving the Traffic Problem.

SOLVING THE
PARKING
PROBLEM

"But, Hubert, dear, how will we ever know which is ours?"
"Patience, dear, we shall plant a tree."

*"Oh, yes! Something
in the suburbs? Say about
the thirty-sixth floor?"*

High Position on Wall Street

"You may quote me as saying: 'I was never so happy in my life as when a youth and poor.'"

"Well, of course, I do say I'll never marry—though, somehow, I've always wanted to be a widow."

"It will rise fifty-five stories into Manhattan skies—a scintillant spire gleaming aureate in the sun's rays—a crowning monument to my career."
"Who's doing the plumbing?"

"What's this I'm reading about your trying to get a divorce from me?"

"Now, dearie, he ain't so bad, really. He ain't stingy an' he's got a big Fiat an' he's gonna drive us down to Princeton for the Yale-Harvard Game."

"Elaine, please remove Floflo. I wish to be alone."

"Poor little girl—to think you've never had anyone to protect you."

A HARVARD MAN ACCEPTS AN INVITATION TO DROP IN AT THE PRINCETON CLUB FOR LUNCH.

THE BORED LADY: *Oh, dear Heaven! Hand it here and I'll kiss it!*

"Well, how's Connecticut?"
"All right, but it gets dark awfully early up there these days."

"Where did you say you went to college?"
"I went to Oxford."
"Oh—that's where you got that lovely Harvard accent."

"My dear, he's absolutely thrilling! Wherever did you find him?"
"Oh, he's an import."

"And then, my dears, Mr. Ruth came to bat and
hit it far into an adjoining field."

"The trouble wit Coolidge is he don't
seem to read the editorials."

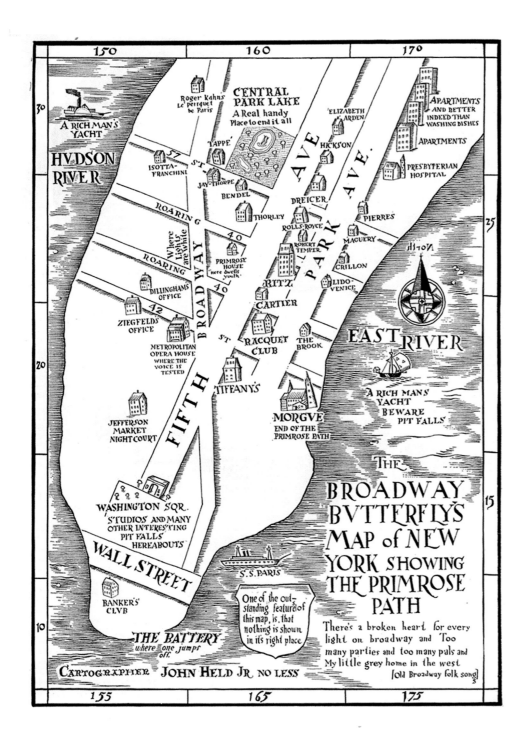

THE

BROADWAY
BUTTERFLY'S
MAP of NEW
YORK SHOWING
THE PRIMROSE
PATH

There's a broken heart for every light on broadway and Too many parties and too many pals and My little grey home in the west [old Broadway folk song]

CARTOGRAPHER JOHN HELD Jr NO LESS

"Y'know, Jawn, the older I get, the more and more do I miss a college education."

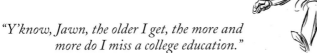

"My! It's nice to get out after being cooped up all day."

"Don't you find the days really too short to start anything serious?"

". . . and don't go beyond W, Harold!"

"Oop—sorry."

"What service! That janitor's forgotten
to sweep the sidewalk again."

29

"*Funny gritting cards? Yez mam, we got
funny gritting cards. Oi yes mam—all day lung
am I in convulzions in mine own store!*"

REHEARSING THE COUGHERS BEFORE
A BROADWAY OPENING

"*I too am really an idealist, my dear,
but life has been very cruel to me.*"

"Whoops! Hand me a brick, dearie—there's a blinkin' Channel swimmer right under us."

"Good God, woman! Think of the social structure!"

"Oh, dear me— Autumn!"

"Say, Doc, do me a favor. Just keep your eye on Consolidated Can Common, and if she goes bearish tell my broker to sell and get four thousand shares of P. & Q. Rails Preferred on the usual margin. Thanks."

1928

*"The trouble is, Madam, most women pay
so little attention to nail health."*

"Pardon me, officer, can you tell me where they moved Hudson Street?"

"Evangeline! That is not the way to try on a coat."

*"Darling, here's the bill from the hospital. One more
installment and the baby's ours."*

"Now, remember—the minute I give the date of Shelley's birth, Benton drops back for a kick."

"Pardon me, sir, but are you one of us?"

"Say, Mrs. Van Sant, the exterminator's here."

"Stop me if you've heard this one."

"Boo! You pretty creature!"

*"Prince Ardalion Lvov Aleksandr Feodor
Hich Sergyeevich Imanoff, and wife."*

"May I assist you, madam?"
"No—I'm just on my way
to the religious books."

"You're so kind to me, and I'm so tired of it all."

"Lord, will you ever learn to close that door behind you? In and out,
in and out—never have I seen such absent-mindedness."

THE DEPRESSION

"But father, do you think I ought to go to work when there's so much unemployment?"

Just around the corner

In 1929, the trading floor of the New York Stock Exchange was just a few subway stops away from *The New Yorker's* midtown offices, but when, in October, the crash came the magazine did its very best to ignore it. Although revenues fell, *The New Yorker's* livelihood was never threatened; Harold Ross's fledgling publication found an audience even in the darkest days. Not that financial absurdity was new to the magazine's cartoonists, who had plenty of fun with the boom of the twenties, and who seem to have noticed that the economy had lost its connection to reality before the market did. A June, 1929, Leonard Dove drawing shows a scion of industry trying to keep his commitment to leisure despite signs that times are getting bad; in another Dove panel, after the collapse, a man suggests that the market may have got what it had coming. And in 1932 Alfred Frueh created the definitive graphic depiction of the financial fall. Cartoonists were, on the whole, less interested in the contrasts between rich and poor than in the way the rich reacted to the crisis; a businessman in a 1930 Carl Rose panel deprives his wife (or mistress?) of a sable. Ironically, the best-remembered cartoon image of the Depression—the despondent broker perched on a ledge, ready to jump—didn't appear in *The New Yorker* until 1960.

"Well, I'm all for putting the Stock Exchange in its place."

"I never told her about the Depression. She would have worried."

"—and you ask for sables."

"Now, you take this depression."
"Huh? What depression?"

*"Don't you think, Doctor, in view of my marked improvement,
I might resume my affection for my mother?"*

"Mrs. Cox, this is my first-born."

*"You know damn well what I want for Christmas!
I told you last Saturday at Looser's."*

"Yes, Mrs. Weatherbee, magnificent animal."

"Yes, dear, I guess I am a little old-fashioned."

"Come on, Al, that's not getting you anywhere."

1929

"Don't keep pulling your skirts over your knees, Aunt Lou. It dates you."

"What'll I do with it now?"

"Yes, in the film version it's a woman—in the book it's a gunboat."

"Yeah, once break the ice wit' Joisey this way
and there's no tellin' what'll happen."

"Come now, you must thank Uncle William
for the nice million dollars."

"And did you have a nice time on your honeymoon?"
"Oh, wonderful! And I met the darlingest man."

1929

"Howard! Have you any ideas on how you want me this evening?"

"We want to report a stolen car."

"Is there anything in the 'Times'?"

"Where's the Southhampton news—Tom, are you sitting on the society section?"

"You got a tree in this yard.
It ain't every house got a tree in its yard."

"I get funny ideas, too, but
I guess I lack the graphic
impulse."

"Yoo hoo! I'm on your side."

"Not now, Junior. Some other time maybe."

"Now see here, Ira! You paid for the trip to Chinatown!"

"No, Bill, I can't marry you. I care only for the abstract in art."

"Something is stifling me—I think it's Mencken."

"All right—all right! I'll shut up—sick as I am—"

"Gives the impression of height, doesn't it?"

"I get so sick of sayin' 'cawn't' all day I could scream."

"Avez-vous 'Ulysses'?"

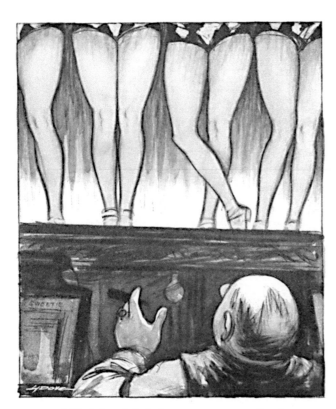

"All right, girls, let's see some personality."

"Tip over?"

"Couldn't you send us a nice, good-looking radical—who isn't too upsetting?"

"My God, we're out of gin!"

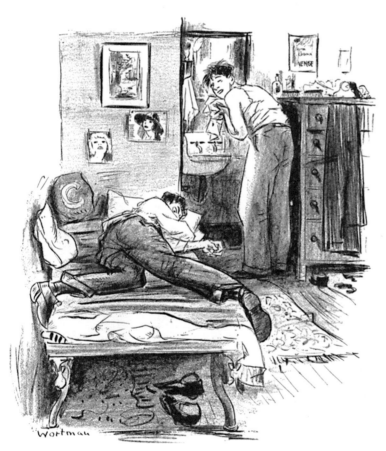

"Why take it so hard—there's lots of other girls in the world, aren't there?"
"I know, but what am I going to do tonight?"

"Good Lord! Here comes that impossible yak again!"

47

"I think I'll take the murder."

*"Er—is that you, Gwendolyn? I believe
this is our dance, Gwendolyn."*

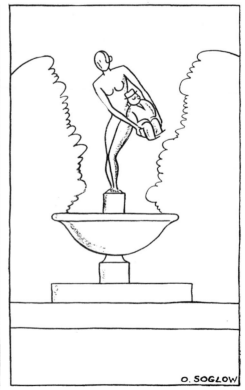

*"Beer at lunch always
makes me drowsy."*

*"My dear child! You don't want a divorce just yet—
wait until the right man comes along."*

*"Why, Henry Whipple, I thought you
were still in medical college!"*

"Well, we can't start till we get that robin out of there."

"Hey, Dad, look, will ya? Before you start
that second movement!"

"Now, stop and think a minute—did _I_ bite you?"

"You great big man! Where've you been all my life?"
"Oswego."

"Oh, the hell with it!"

"Get Mamma a needle and thread like a good boy,
and don't stand there gaping!"

1931

"The minute I saw this carp, Mrs. Mugler, I thought of you."

"Don't you see, Ma! Columbia wins twenty-seven to nothing!"

"The Waldorf!"

"Isn't that that friend of Father's?"

"And so to bed—eh, old man?"

O. SOGLOW

"Now we'll know what's what."

"Well, stupid, don't just sit there."

"*He doesn't seem to have got much yet out of his three months at Yale.*"

"*They haven't got a single tenant on the fifty-fourth floor yet, Mr. Chrysler.*"

"*I don't object to passion if it's treated with dignity.*"

"What other bad words do you know?"

"Oh, George,
you daredevil!
You frighten me."

"Henry, you _must_ see this!"
"Describe it to me."

"I've gotten sort of tired of it."

"Pardon me, Miss Plunkett."

"I can tell you right now that isn't going to work."

"Follow that sunset!"

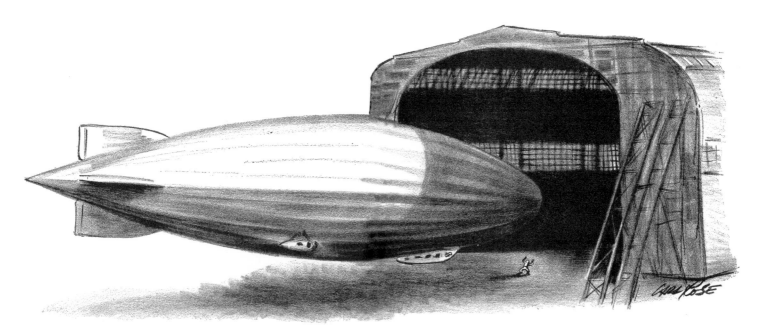

"Back 'er up another foot, Cap, and cut 'er hard to the left."

"Will somebody pick a card, any card?"

"Now can you hear me—you boys in the back?"

"You're fired!"

"All right, have it your way—you heard a seal bark!"

"I'd rather not go out right after a bath."

"Very clever, sir. Brilliant satire."

"Hey, is Frank up there?"
"Wait and I'll look and see."

"Fundamentally the ship was sound."

O. SOGLOW

"Malcolm! She wants you."

Robt. Day

*"Couldn't you keep your ideals and
still be in the fur business?"*

"Say, what time do we get to Albany?"

"Touché!"

"Psst, Marge. Quit shooting to her backhand—
she'll never ask us out again."

61

1932

"Well, you suggest something then!"

"Awfully nice of you to ask me to stay."

"Make a nice foreclosure, wouldn't it?"

"Her parties get worse every year."

"...Hello, Edmund. Hello, Warwick. Hello, Teddy.
Hello, Poodgie. Hello, Kip. Hello, Freddie..."

O ne day in 1925, with *The New Yorker* struggling to reach its first birthday, a tall, good-looking young man strolled into the magazine's offices with a large portfolio of sketches. The drawings—funny, exuberant, and Jazz Age risqué—had exactly the attitude that Harold Ross was trying to establish in his new magazine. Even better, the artist, Peter Arno, Yale dropout and son of a prominent New York judge, was a member of just the audience of smart, well-to-do young people Ross was trying to reach. Arguably, the well-reported escapades of this dashing young man about town did as much, at first, for the reputation of *The New Yorker* as his drawings.

Cartooning, it turned out, was not Arno's only strength. He played jazz piano, wrote and produced a Broadway show, and was a widely published journalist. He designed the coat in his closet and the car in his garage. Perhaps out of sheer exhaustion, he relied on gag writers for a steady supply of ideas for his drawings. Many of his best-remembered lines and characters, including the mysterious Whoops Sisters, were conceived by Philip Wylie, Ross's Man Friday; by Richard McAllister, a regular gag writer; or by James Geraghty, who became the magazine's art editor in 1939.

For all Arno's energy, his style matured at a leisurely pace. The freewheeling sketches he drew in the nineteen-twenties, clearly influenced by Daumier, didn't give way to his signature work—brilliantly lit, boldly outlined dioramas sculpted with exquisitely chosen washes—until the mid-thirties. These drawings, with their plutocrats, chorus girls, and outraged matrons, often ran as full pages and occasionally as double-page spreads. Though they were rendered in black-and-white, their richness and luminosity brought a strong sense of depth to the magazine's pages. Arno continued to publish in *The New Yorker* until his death, in 1968.

By that time, he had long since abandoned the bright lights of Manhattan for the skies of Westchester County. Arno's reputation as a hell-raiser remained intact, however. When reporters asked Arno's daughter, Patricia, for anecdotes about her father, she replied, "None are repeatable."

"You're a mystic, Mr. Ryan. All Irishmen are mystics."

"Valerie won't be around for several days.
She backed into a sizzling platter."

"Makes you kind of pleased to be an American, doesn't it?"

1933

"Hey, wake up! I'm a prospect!"

"I'm sorry, Madam, but if that's a dog, it's not allowed."

*"On and on they came! I pulled the switch and the
whole circus train was wrecked."*

"I saw it all coming ten years ago."

"For gosh sakes, here comes Mrs. Roosevelt!"

"Mind if I show my cow around?"

1933

"I love coffee, I love tea. I love the girls, an' the girls love me."

"He pointed out how it's our depression, not just yours and mine."

"The upswing will come. It'll come. This can't go on!"

"How long have you been up there?"

"Are you the motion-picture reviewer of this newspaper?"

1933

"I shall now quote the passages which I consider obscene."

"Sh, Darling. Daddy's afraid he'll have to work in New Jersey!"

"Why, Hobart! We're quarrelling!"

"I tell you there isn't going to be any insurrection."

LIFE CLASS IN A NUDIST COLONY

"Do you take this woman to be your
lawful wedded wife?"

71

"Let's give Jimmie Adams a ring. Maybe he can think of something to do."

"Mr. Calkins takes you on to here, Madam, and then we put you in Mr. Samson's hands."

"Here you are, folks. Are you interested in recapturing the glamour of a vanished era?"

"Do you think I like to steal?"

"En garde—keel me or I keel you!"

"We're on a budget."

"If you can keep a secret, I'll tell you how my husband died."

"Oh, she's been acting that way all day. Someone
told her she looks like Katharine Hepburn."

"Hey, what about dames?"

"That's right, stupid—drop 'em all over the lot!"

"Mamma, there's a lot of people in my bed."

"My man don't wrestle till we hear it talk."

"You're getting warmer."

"It'll be a few minutes before we can shoot.
You folks want something to eat?"

"Pardon me, Madame, is Cook's this way?"

"Now, for heaven's sake, dear, think back. <u>Where</u> did you put the yacht when you left Kennebunkport?"

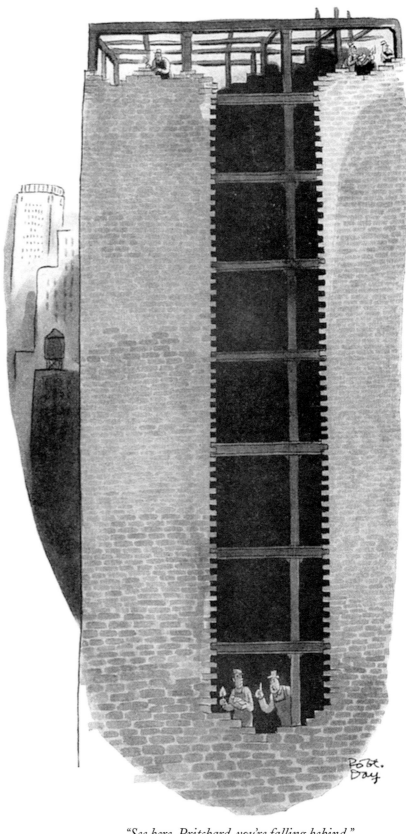

"See here, Pritchard, you're falling behind."

"Startin' kinda early, ain't we?"

"Of course it's much too early to draw conclusions.
The Harvard entrance examinations will tell the story."

"Perhaps we ought to set up some
simple form of government."

"Professor Furbush has been telling me about the N'gambi fertility rites— and guess what they turn out to be!"

"The other side! My God, the water's supposed to be on the other side."

"Oswald's getting pretty conservative lately."

"Well, back to the old drawing board."

THE SECOND DECADE
1935-1944

THE *SECOND* DECADE
1935-1944

NANCY FRANKLIN

"If this doesn't get us in, nothing will."

"I suppose all that you men think about is war."

Ever since I started working at *The New Yorker*, people have made a point of telling me, as they stand there swirling their drink, that the first thing they do when a new issue of the magazine arrives is to look at the cartoons. They nearly always make this declaration in a defiant tone, as if they expected to have to defend the practice. But who would argue with their priorities? The readers of *The New Yorker* who work at the magazine love the cartoons just as much as the readers who don't.

I suspect that there have been Cartoon Firsters since the twenties (although they would have had to wait until 1930, when cellophane tape was invented, to be able to paper their iceboxes with their favorite drawings), and certainly by the mid-thirties, by which time *The New Yorker*, having started out as a shaky enterprise, editorially and financially, was both in the pink and in the black, even as the country's fortunes were falling. (The magazine's flushness was due in no small part to the repeal of Prohibition, in December of 1933. Within minutes, *The New Yorker* was swimming in liquor advertising.)

The years from 1935 through 1944 were fertile ones at the magazine. The decade was Thurber's most productive period, his war between men and women not slowed for a minute by the Second World War; Helen Hokinson published more than seven hundred cartoons, all of them—yes, all of them—winning and funny to this day; and Arno's style reached its bold, bawdy apotheosis. In 1941, Saul Steinberg began appearing in the magazine; while on special assignment with the Office of Strategic Services, he sent in visual dispatches from Europe, North Africa, and Asia. In 1940, one of the best-known cartoons in the magazine's history appeared: Charles Addams's captionless drawing of a skier going downhill, his tracks in the snow making it appear that he has gone neither *through* a tree behind him, exactly, nor *around* it, exactly, but in some way both. Not possible? Look at the drawing.

Though by the late twenties *The New Yorker* had a large national circulation, its outlook was still, by design, local; its mission was to illustrate, in words and pictures, the ins and outs, highs and lows, of the mecca of culture, commerce, and consumerism. (In a 1938 Mary Petty cartoon, two men sit across a desk from each other with a book manuscript between them, and one says, "Then everything is settled but the television and doll rights.") *The New Yorker*, Harold Ross wrote, "will not be iconoclastic," and it wasn't. In some quarters, this world view, this tolerance—or promotion—of smart-set mores, was sharply criticized. Dwight Macdonald, writing in 1937 in *Partisan Review*, deplored the magazine's "Jovian aloofness from the common struggle. In times like these there is something monstrously inhuman in the deliberate cultivation of the trivial." It is true that the magazine largely ignored the Depression, and it was not jostling for position when it came to political movements. The satirical cartoons often took a sidelong approach to their subjects, yet their touch was distinct and sure, and no less pointed for being light. They weren't trivial, no matter how apparently small their subject, unless you make the mistake of thinking that humor and seriousness are always unrelated opposites. In addition to delivering weekly pleasure to our door, the cartoons throw open a window onto the history of our imaginations and desires and preoccupations, and onto those of the artists who drew them. (And, of course, the cartoons provide an invaluable translation service: how else would we know what our dogs and cats are saying to each other?)

There are some notable oddities in the cartoons of the era. (The racial and ethnic stereotypes in some of the old cartoons are not oddities as such—they were too widespread in the culture to count as oddities.) For example, there are proportionally more cartoons about the 1939 World's Fair, which lasted a mere year and a half, than there are about Franklin Roosevelt, whose Presidency spanned this entire period. Ross, apparently, was quite taken with the exposition, perhaps because it was in the magazine's back yard, and one could make a case that, editorially speaking, he stayed too long at the fair. Around the same time, though—even before the war began in Europe, and well before the draft began here, in 1940—the magazine's cartoonists were transmuting the nervousness in the air and the rumblings on the ground into works on paper.

But it doesn't do justice to the cartoons in this book to categorize them by their subjects, even when they fall into familiar genres: the singleton or duo on a desert island, two guys in a bar, the boss bitelessly barking at his (rarely "her") secretary over the intercom. Each is unique, a one-time-only amazement. People often ask cartoonists how or where they get their ideas; it's a natural question, and it's also one that can't be answered. The truth of the matter is that the best *New Yorker* cartoons can't be reduced to words. They're easy to pin up, and impossible to pin down.

"Then everything is settled but the television and doll rights."

"Aren't we going to toot?"

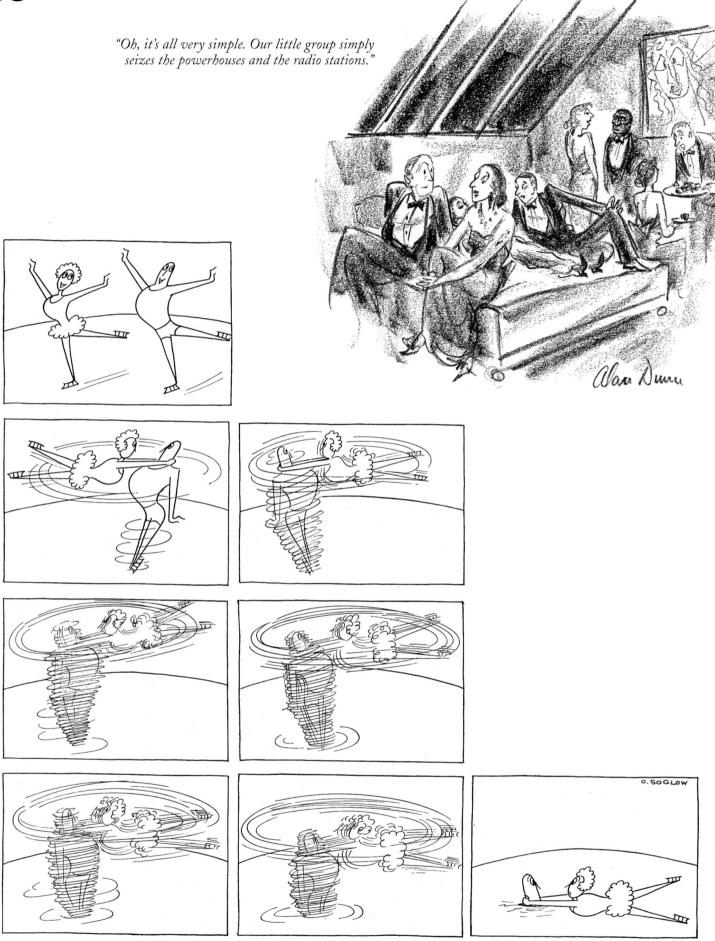

"Oh, it's all very simple. Our little group simply seizes the powerhouses and the radio stations."

"No, no, no! I just wanted the room tinted a light buff."

"It's a real Mohammedan prayer rug. Of course, _we_ just use it for decoration."

"If my calculations are correct, you will soon be playing third base for the Detroit Tigers."

Tattle-Tale

Bully

Peeping Tom

Pyromaniac

Liar

SMALL FRY
CRIMINAL TYPES

• •

Sadist

Cheat

"I told him there are some things I won't do, and going to museums is one of them."

"One for you, one for me, one for the Museum of Natural History."

"Oh, birdman!"

"Now, in this scene, Franz Schubert, the composer, falls asleep and dreams his melody while the girls dance it out on the piano keys. Get it?"

"Rheinbeck! It's Grandmamma!"

"Well, pay me! He ate it."

"That's my first wife up there, and this is the <u>present</u> Mrs. Harris."

"Good heavens, can't I turn my back on you for a minute?"

"This one is a little cheaper. There's a curse on it."

"The vote is now fifteen to one that we deplore Mussolini's attitude. I think it would be nice if we could go on record as <u>unanimously</u> deploring Mussolini's attitude."

"You wanted to see Santa Claus and you're <u>going</u> to see him!"

"I can't go ashore. I haven't any pants on."

91

1936

A CARAVAN OF CALIFORNIA MILLIONAIRES, FLEEING EASTWARD FROM THE STATE INCOME TAX, ENCAMPS FOR THE NIGHT IN HOSTILE WISCONSIN TERRITORY

"Come on, get hot!"

"Rubbish! Lots of children are unwanted. Your father and I didn't want you."

"That ogle, Mr. Bentinck—is that natural?"

"Approach, women of Athens!"

"You'll have to excuse me.
I'm all thumbs today."

"Hey, Mr. Raboldi! Surprise!"

"If my wife's on that boat, just pretend you don't know me."

"Be sure to get back in time for dinner."

"Well, tomorrow's our first anniversary. How about having some of the gang in to buck us up?"

1936

"Excuse me, Mr. President, _this_ button opens Boulder Dam—_that_ button is Mr. McIntyre."

"Jackson has been with us so long he's just like one of the family."

"Go away, Edith! You confuse me."

"Congratulations, sir. You've hit the jackpot."

"Come along. We're going to the
Trans-Lux to hiss Roosevelt."

"I don't care what you say—I'm cold!"

"No, no, Harvey, not their faces—just the windshield!"

"Don't just stand there—get witnesses!"

"I can't smell a thing, either."

"He just bought all we had and gave them their freedom."

"We just missed him. It's still warm."

"It's nothing at all, really—just an old mutilated torso."

"Madam, Mr. Robert has returned from Hotchkiss."

*"It's a naïve domestic Burgundy without any breeding,
but I think you'll be amused by its presumption."*

"I imagine it's the University of Southern California."

"But I thought I had another, an older one."

1937

"Tell 'em to dump their industrials. Further details later."

"I hear war may be declared any day now."

*"This is the round that starts them weeping
for the Spanish Loyalists."*

"Oh, let's declare war and get the whole damn thing over with."

1937

"Dear no, Miss Mayberry—just the head."

*"Armbruster here has what I think is
a marvellous suggestion."*

"Today Mr. Chatfield is going to show us a little—
but not *too* much—of the horror in Spain."

"Which would be the most restful—go to the
movies and then have dinner, or have dinner
and then go to the movies?"

"Telephone, Mr. Pritchett."

"Well, if I called the wrong number, why did you answer the phone?"

THE MASCULINE APPROACH

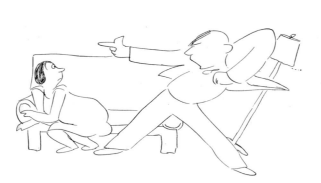

The You'll-Never-See-Me-Again Tactics

The Heroic, or Dangers-I-Have-Known, Method

The Let-'Em-Wait-and-
Wonder Plan

college work with no grade below
was elected to Sigma Delta Chi, honorary
journalism fraternity. I have also been ma-
joring in Elizabethan drama, and in my junior
year, I was editor of our college literary
monthly.

I should, therefore, appreciate hearing
from you regarding any openings you may have
on your reportorial staff, especially in your
dramatic department. I stand ready to depart
for New York on a few hours notice, in the
event of a favorable reply.

Thanking you for any consideration you may
give this application, I remain,

                                    Sincerely yo

"My wife is sort of a back-seat driver, you know."

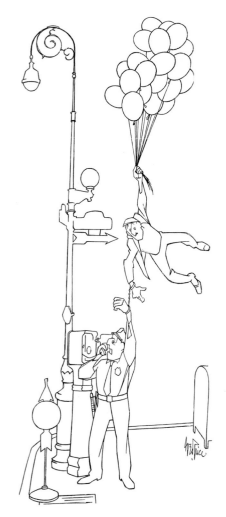

"*Vending without a license—
and get over here quick!*"

"*Damn it, I am looking pleasant!*"

George Price's repertory company of sourballs, misfits, and losers did not spring full-blown from the artist's head. They were inspired, Price always insisted, by eccentric neighbors and friends in his tiny home town of Coytesville, New Jersey.

For someone with such raw material, a career as a cartoonist would seem to have been inevitable. In fact, he got his start in advertising and was making his living as a freelance illustrator when he was lured into cartoons, reluctantly, by *The New Yorker's* promise to supply him with gag ideas. (Such collaboration was not unusual; in the thirties, few cartoonists worked with their own ideas.)

Price's formidable skills as a draftsman were honed during sketching trips with the social-realist painter George (Pop) Hart, one of his father's friends. (Hart also introduced Price to older cartoonists, including George Herriman, the creator of Krazy Kat.) Price's energetic, sinuous line, whether rendered in brush or pen, evokes the spontaneity of his boyhood sketches. But his cartoons were as carefully constructed as architectural blueprints. He would submit "preliminary" sketches that were as fully worked out as his finishes; the only difference was that the former were drawn in pencil on tracing paper while the latter were rendered in India ink on bristol board.

Price was a man of strong opinions, and he didn't mind sharing them. He loathed do-gooders and politicians. While he could be generous toward his fellow-artists, he was just as often dismissive; he gave Arno and Booth high marks, but claimed that the work of Norman Rockwell—whom he called "that cutie"—made him physically ill.

Over a sixty-year career at *The New Yorker*, Price produced more than twelve hundred cartoons but just one cover, for the issue of December 25, 1965. Set in a New York subway car, it depicts a downcast gaggle of Santas resolutely commuting to the city's department stores.

This was one comic idea that Price dreamed up completely on his own, and, to use another of his favorite phrases, "It was a beaut!"

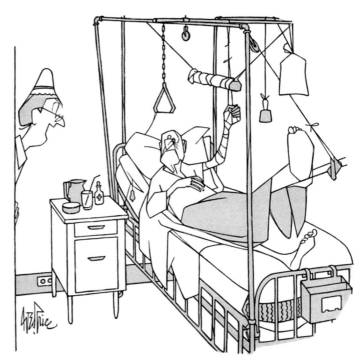

"Have your pillows been plumped this morning?"

"Here's the guest room. Just make yourselves at home."

"Er—haven't you forgotten something?"

"You and your premonitions!"

"Why, Harriet, I hardly recognized you!"

"I beg your pardon, but I
think you're sitting on my eyelashes."

"Most successful suit sale we ever had, I should say."

"Any minute now we're due for one of his
outbursts of gloomy philosophy."

"This one seems about the right size."

"I don't think you've quite caught its sweep, its limitless expanse, its sheer bigness."

"Better hold it. Here's another memo from Mr. De Mille."

"Well, folks, here it is starting time. . . One moment while
we take a look at that little old schedule."

"Harry isn't in."

"I know it's quitting time, but I can't disappoint a crowd like that."

"I beg your pardon. Did you say 'Rover'?"

"Why, Richard Honeywell, I believe you're jealous."

"You certainly had me worried. Your horse came back without you."

"Sure-footed little beasts, aren't they?"

"Through the Tenth Dynasty to the Ming porcelain, turn
right at the Italian Renaissance, and you'll see a little door."

"No, no, McNamara. Just that white fluffy stuff on top."

"Take it, Andrew!"

"You wait here and I'll bring the etchings down."

"Next?"

"You certainly have a peculiar sense of humor."

"And now, ladies and gentlemen, our dream of eighteen years has come true."

"The hell of it is I've forgotten what they're reaching for."

"O.K., Maria. You can put on the chops now."

"If it gives you any more trouble, let me know."

"I'm sorry, Herr General, but this man says
we've already conquered his country."

1939

"I suppose to a sailor that would have some significance."

"Tell me more about your husband, Mrs. Briggs."

"Watch out, Fred! Here it comes again!"

"A table near the door, sir, in the event
of a national emergency?"

"Here comes the mother, ladies and gentlemen and,
boy, is she burned up about something."

"Well that's how it is, men. You just
rub two dry sticks together."

"And how does everybody want their eggs this morning?"

"There's a burglar prowling about in the Blue Room, sir.
Would you care to have a crack at him before I call the police?"

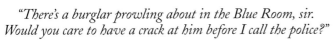

"Cut it, Dolan! Remember we're in uniform."

"Straight ahead. You can't miss it!"

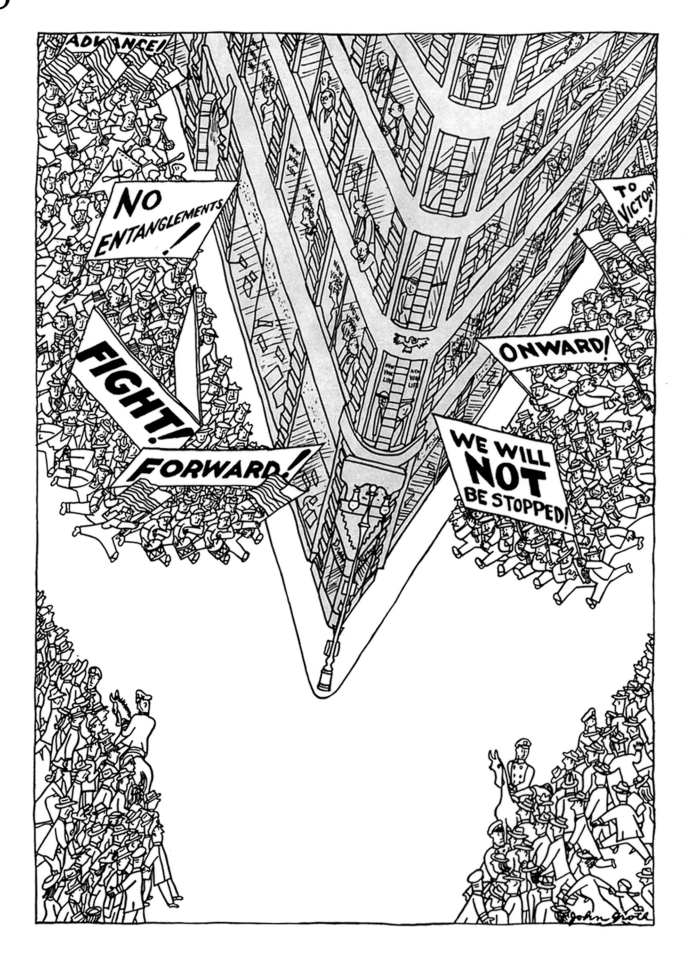

"Which one is the love potion?"

"All right, men, break step."

"He's out."

THE WAR AT HOME

Abreast of the news

Preparedness

Orphan

Assistant G-Man

Isolationist

"Now read me the part again where I disinherit everybody."

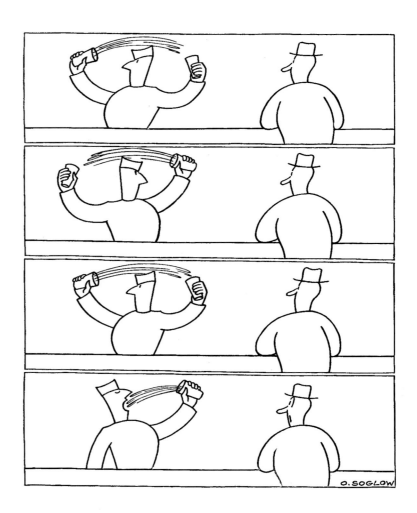

"Does this ticket entitle me to a hangover in Philadelphia?"

"We forgot to bring the children!"

"Boy, did _I_ have an afternoon! The census man was here."

"Well, here's where I say good night."

"I'm through with the paper, Roberts. Take it out and sell it."

"The most convenient method is to use a simple,
inexpensive cigarette lighter."

Dog meat has been eaten in every major German crisis
at least since the time of Frederick the Great, and
is commonly referred to as "blockade mutton." It is

tough, gamy, strong-flavored.
—*Time, November 25th.*

1941

"Daddy, can I have the tickets to tear up?"

"Not yet, Michael. They're just tuning up."

"Why, you poor child! You're running right over to Brooks Brothers."

"Wherever Hartwell goes, he tries to make at least one new friend."

"He wants to know if he may make a small sacrifice in front of it."

1941

"It'll go faster, dear, if you rake them in piles, and __then__ burn them."

"Hey, Montgomery! Hands up!"

"I'm sure Baby's in here somewhere."

"Blunt instruments?"

*"Wouldn't it be a smart move, Jim, for us to
lay in a supply of money?"*

*"The sponsors of this news broadcast, Clarkson & Sons,
makers of the world-famous Clarkson Chicken Noodle Soup
Mix, the soup prepared from an old Maryland recipe and
endorsed by twelve of the country's leading chefs and which can
be made so quickly and economically—simply add the hot water
and there you are!—forego their usual sales message in order to
bring you complete news coverage during this emergency."*

"Uh—do I have to do anything?"

"You needn't wait, Benson. I'll be some time."

CUSTOM TAILORS

PARK HERE

BAR & GRILL

SANDWICH

BEER

"Now, boys, this is what we call a drunk."

New Yorker cartoonists never gave up on drinking—not even during Prohibition, when bootleggers, bartenders, and drunks were regular figures in the pages of the magazine. Once the ban was lifted, in 1933, many of the cartoon figures seem to have been soused as often as not. Few cartoonists of the time allowed drunks to speak for themselves, however. Instead, the drunks are cautiously approached by waitresses, tossed out by bartenders, or tolerated by their employers. Even the woman who, in Barbara Sherman's 1937 cartoon, calls a friend to suggest a day of debauchery does so with a comic sobriety. James Thurber was the one cartoonist who consistently violated this rule, drawing a tipsy woman hallucinating owls, a sloshed matron threatening her guests with full disclosure, and even an otherwise demure wife crawling across the floor while under the influence. But it is an apparently sober woman who, in a 1938 cartoon by Shermund, sitting in a canoe with her friend, issues the final word on alcohol as a social lubricant.

"Of course I couldn't tell much about him.
Both times I met him he was sober."

"There isn't much we can do about it. She's simply
marvellous with the children."

"Sober, Mrs. Tomkins is the personification of virtue."

"We got all the children off to school today. Would you and
Fred be interested in going out and getting plastered?"

"Wouldn't you care to eat something now, sir?"

137

*"Of course, if they don't bomb Sutton Place,
I'm going to look like a damn fool."*

"Do much walking?"

"Your being a vegetarian certainly takes a load off my mind."

"What sort of a job?"

"Tough luck! And your briefcase arm, too."

"It started with some awfully good repartee."

"Have you an appointment?"

"I think I may say, without fear of contradiction . . ."

"Of course, if <u>he</u> leaves for a defense job we're licked."

"Damn it. I came here to forget the war!"

"I want to report a tornado."

"Madge?"

"I tell you, Mamma, the blood keeps going to my head."

"This ought to be good."

"Quicksand or not, Barclay, I've half a mind to struggle."

"I just got damn well fed up with being formal all the time."

"I'm sorry, but there's nothing for you now. And what's more, I'm not at all sure we'll be hiring men after the war."

"Look at it this way—you're the baby sparrow and I'm the mamma sparrow."

"That's the younger generation for you—absolutely no regard for tradition."

"Professor Merton is a brilliant man in his field,
but he has absolutely no small talk."

"If I made any mistakes, will I be sent to the Big House?"

"Still, did you ever stop to think where you and
I would be if it weren't for evil?"

145

1943

"Oh, don't worry about Charlie—
he's the tail gunner."

"Now, what did we make before we got all
these government contracts?"

1944

"Isn't he cunning? He feels guilty about something."

"We're looking for something that's also edible."

148

"I don't care _who_ started it."

"I am afraid that Professer Witherspoon has erred in his quotation of Verlaine. That line, if memory serves, goes rather like this. . ."

"Their first reaction is one of fright and hysteria. Then a strange apathy seems to seize them and they lose the will to live."

"Haven't you anything nonmilitary? Herbert is more interested in the postwar world."

DREAMS OF GLORY

"Guess what happened to me and the truck, boss!...
No.... No.... No, guess again."

"Ouch, sir."

"I always give them the best of care, lady. Politics don't enter into it."

"Collaborationists, probably."

"I'm sorry, but none of these are quite like the one I saw in my dreams."

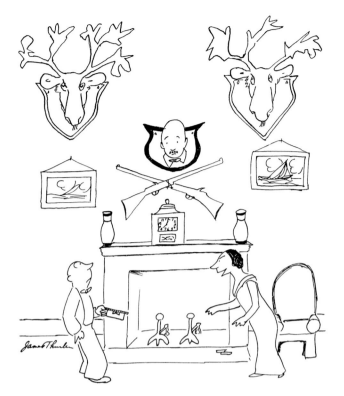

"Let me take your hat, Mr. Williams."

"The father belonged to some people who were driving through in a Packard."

James Thurber might be called *The New Yorker's* accidental cartoonist. Thurber joined the editorial staff in 1927—he wrote regularly for The Talk of the Town—and shared a pocket-size office with his friend and mentor, E. B. White. Between bouts at the typewriter, Thurber littered the space with sketches of his favorite subjects: men, women, and dogs. (He also drew on the walls, fragments of which were removed from the magazine's original premises and are now displayed in the *New Yorker's* current offices.)

White found Thurber's doodles irresistible and, after adding appropriate captions, attempted to persuade Harold Ross to publish them. Ross, aware of Thurber's taste for practical jokes, believed that his leg was being pulled—these weren't his idea of proper cartoons—and refused. It was only after reviewers of the White-Thurber collaboration "Is Sex Necessary?" (1929) praised Thurber's drawings that Ross relented. (Ross even became a bit of a fan; hearing Thurber described as a "fifth-rate artist," he replied, firmly, "Third-rate!")

This collection includes, for the first time since "The Seal in the Bedroom" (1932), all of Thurber's captioned cartoons for the magazine—almost four hundred, covering twenty-five years. Many of these, of course, have become part of that secret code by which *New Yorker* buffs identify themselves: "Ooooo, *guesties!*"

The English painter Paul Nash, one of Thurber's earliest boosters, compared his drawings to Matisse's. This may seem like a stretch, but it's certainly true that the elegant abandon of his style decisively freed cartooning from its roots in traditional illustration. Thurber was blind by the time he died, in 1961, but he never gave up on humor, or on writing. (To some readers, in fact, he is better known for his written work, which includes such stories as "The Secret Life of Walter Mitty.") Thurber's cartoons are, of course, uniquely his own, but they also created a template for much of the work in today's *New Yorker*. His minimalist style and seamless blend of caption and drawing provided the pedigree for a new generation of artist-writers, including Bruce Eric Kaplan, David Sipress, and Roz Chast.

"Perhaps _this_ will refresh your memory."

"I don't know them either, dear, but there may be
some very simple explanation."

THE WAR BETWEEN MEN AND WOMEN
XI. Zero Hour—Connecticut

THE THIRD DECADE
1945-1954

THE THIRD DECADE
1945-1954

LILLIAN ROSS

"Mr. Mitchell! You __know__ you don't have kitchen privileges."

In 1945, I discovered the comic art of *The New Yorker*, experiencing pleasurable shock, wonder, laughter, and relief, finally, in finding some diversion from the agonies of the Second World War and its aftermath: Peter Arno's white-mustached, tuxedo-clad, sex-hungry Lotharios; William Steig's lovable "Small Fry" and his satirically hectoring wives; the wonderfully drawn Charles Addams characters (landlady to frazzled man putting his head in the oven: "Mr. Mitchell! You *know* you don't have kitchen privileges"). Front-page events in those years were overwhelming. In early 1945, President Roosevelt was conferring with Joseph Stalin and Winston Churchill at Yalta, agreeing that Russia would enter the war against Japan. A couple of months later, F.D.R. died of a cerebral hemorrhage, at the age of sixty-three. And less than a month after that, with Harry S. Truman as President, Germany surrendered. It was comforting to me to mark the closing days of the war by going along with the cartoonists. Alan Dunn's drawing of a "Separation Center": a tough-looking sergeant in uniform carrying his suitcase exits the building, and around the corner stand half a dozen vengeful privates, suitcases at their feet, awaiting him. Mischa Richter's bald, portly officer addressing a bunch of soldiers: "Now, remember. Civilians have been through a lot. Don't try to *make* them talk about their experiences, but if they *want* to talk, let them."

On August 6, 1945, the United States dropped the bomb on Hiroshima. A year later, John Hersey made journalistic history with the publication of "Hiroshima," in an issue (August 31, 1946) of *The New Yorker* devoted solely to that piece—with no cartoons. But my heart was equally in synch with the cartoons that followed in later issues: Alan Dunn's two soldiers peeling potatoes, with the caption "I thought that bomb was going to revolutionize warfare." Or the Robert J. Day cartoon showing a man setting fire to a trash-can in his back yard, with smoke rising in a mushroom cloud. Or, a few years on, one of Helen Hokinson's ladies taking a question at a meeting of her look-alikes: "But if we disband our Defend America Committee, won't Russia take it as a sign of yielding?"

In the postwar years, Jackie Robinson broke the color barrier in baseball by joining the Brooklyn Dodgers; the Kinsey Report on human sexuality was published; eleven leaders of the Communist Party were convicted of advocating the violent overthrow of the United States government; President Truman authorized the production of the H bomb; the Korean War started; Truman fired General MacArthur from his Korea command; the first hydrogen bomb was exploded in the Pacific; Adlai Stevenson ran for President against Dwight Eisenhower and lost; Senator Joseph McCarthy held televised hearings on Communist influences in the State Department; the Supreme Court ordered that the public schools be integrated with "all deliberate speed." At the same time, *New Yorker* cartoonists continued to find a way to provide lightness and laughter: Garrett Price gave us the clerk in the toy store putting "H" stickers in front of the word "Bomb" on the boxes of "Junior Bomb" sets; Charles Addams gave us a little boy at the sailboat pond, putting a toy submarine in the water and aiming it at the boats; Chon Day gave us the little boy writing on the fence "JIMMY BUTLER IS A COMMUNIST"; Alain gave us the woman in her kitchen saying to the plumber fixing the sink pipes, "In the event of germ warfare, I suppose you'd be among the first alerted"; Carl Rose gave us the group of uniformed officers seated at a military conference table, with the head officer, push button on the table before him, saying, "Now, gentlemen, any practical consideration of push-button warfare must begin with one basic operational technique"; Mary Petty gave us the wealthy couple at a long dinner table, the wife saying, "Has anybody ever thought of winning the Communists over to our way of life?"; and Peter Arno gave us the busty bimbo saying to a panel of males, "I really don't know if he was a Communist. We never discussed politics."

In 1941, Saul Steinberg introduced a wholly new type of comic art to the magazine. One of his earliest cartoons was of a man leading six people to the entrance of a dining room and holding up his hand to the maître d'; the hand had seven fingers. The drawing already displayed his spare, geometric lines. Another early one showed a little boy opening a gift box under a Christmas tree drawn with a multitude of those Steinbergian lines; the box contained a large pocket watch and a hammer. In 1953, he drew a man in a single line, with feet going up to the face, which was turned in the opposite direction. William Shawn, then the magazine's editor, often said to James Geraghty, the art editor, that, in his opinion, Steinberg was one of the two greatest artists of the twentieth century—the other being Picasso.

"Now, remember. Civilians have been through a lot. Don't try to make them talk about their experiences, but if they want to talk, let them."

"Thank you very, very much. I don't know how I can ever repay you."

"May I ask a question? There are still one or two things about the postwar world that bother me."

"That's not necessary here, Madam.
The room clerk will keep it for you."

"I llove you."

"Oh, I couldn't make it Friday—I've so many things
to do. It's the thirteenth, you know."

"Who's in charge here?"

"Has anybody ever thought of winning the
Communists over to _our_ way of life?"

"Do you mind?"

"I suppose in a few years all this will be done by atomic power."

"Wouldn't you love to see this in Technicolor?"

"Still mad?"

"If *I* were my third husband, I know *I'd* try to outshine the others."

"Yours readjusted yet?"

"I hope you don't object to children."

1946

"Maybe he forgot something."

"Albert, how big a standing army do you suppose we'd have to have to stay at peace with the whole world?"

"O.K. now. You got it straight what you're supposed to do?"

"Gee, Jack! That was very careless of you."

"You're _too_ far back now, dear. Come forward a little."

1946

*"I never could tell the difference between
a stalactite and a stalagmite."*

*"We in this business no longer talk of television as being in the
misty realm of things to come. No, sir! The magic of television
has emerged from the laboratory a triumphant reality."*

1946

"When were you built?"

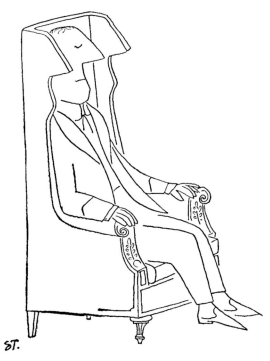

"Of course, we could adopt some."

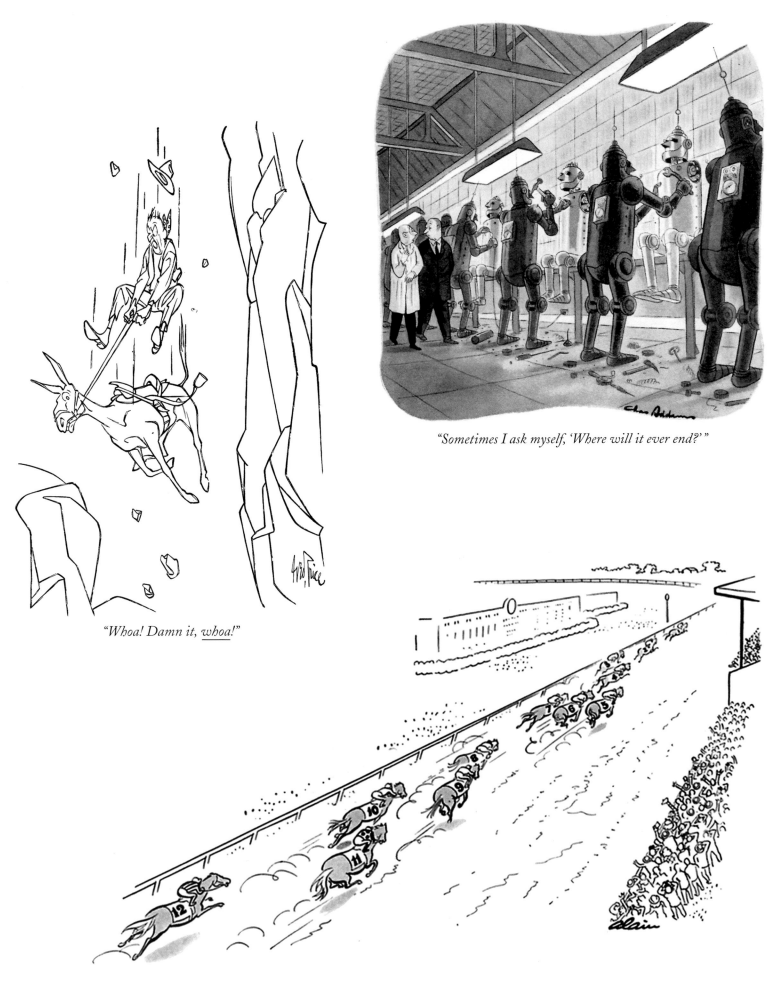

"Whoa! Damn it, <u>whoa!</u>"

"Sometimes I ask myself, 'Where will it ever end?'"

OCCUPANCY BY MORE
THAN 71,699 PERSONS
IS DANGEROUS AND
UNLAWFUL

"The gentleman wants to know if you'd care to
join him in a little argument."

"You have *so* got it turned off!"

175

"When you finish this one, boys, I'd like a word with you over at the office."

"... and never, never go near a house with
a well-beaten path to the door."

"For God's sake, Hortense, where are
my elevator shoes?"

"What's my I.Q. so far?"

"Just look at that Mrs. Owens—cruise clothes!"

1947

O. SOGLOW

STEINBERG

PETER ARNO

"Sometimes we sell them, lady, but only to other teams."

"*They never said what they had against it.*"

1.

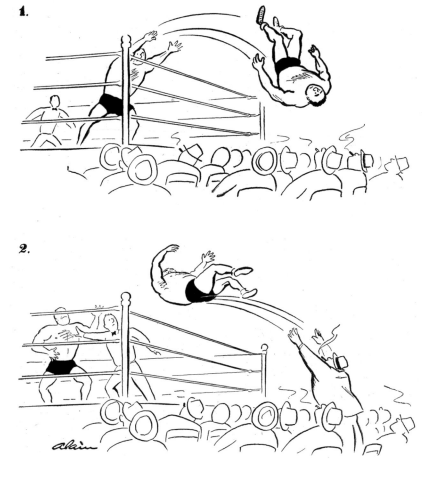

2.

"*Which one? Great heavens, are you mad?*"

*"Since you're going to get a ticket anyway,
how about racing to the overpass?"*

"For goodness' sake! Why didn't they tell us there'd be an extra inning?"

"I didn't say anything. That was yesterday."

"May I suggest, Senator, that perhaps we should just offer the whole five and a half billion to Mr. Stalin to buy off Communism itself?"

"Come in, come in, whoever you are."

"Pardon me, are you using this knee?"

"George! George! Drop the keys!"

"Is there a _Mrs._ Kinsey?"

1948

"Makes you realize how big dams are, doesn't it?"

"Hmm—I don't like the looks of that eye."

"Now, gentlemen, any practical consideration of
push-button warfare must begin with
one basic operational technique."

"I suppose we'll have to set this down as a doubtful district."

"The first thing you must realize is that your inferiority complex is just as good as the next person's."

"Harrison is right. It's a square knot."

"It's awfully kind of you, but I'm trying to give up smoking."

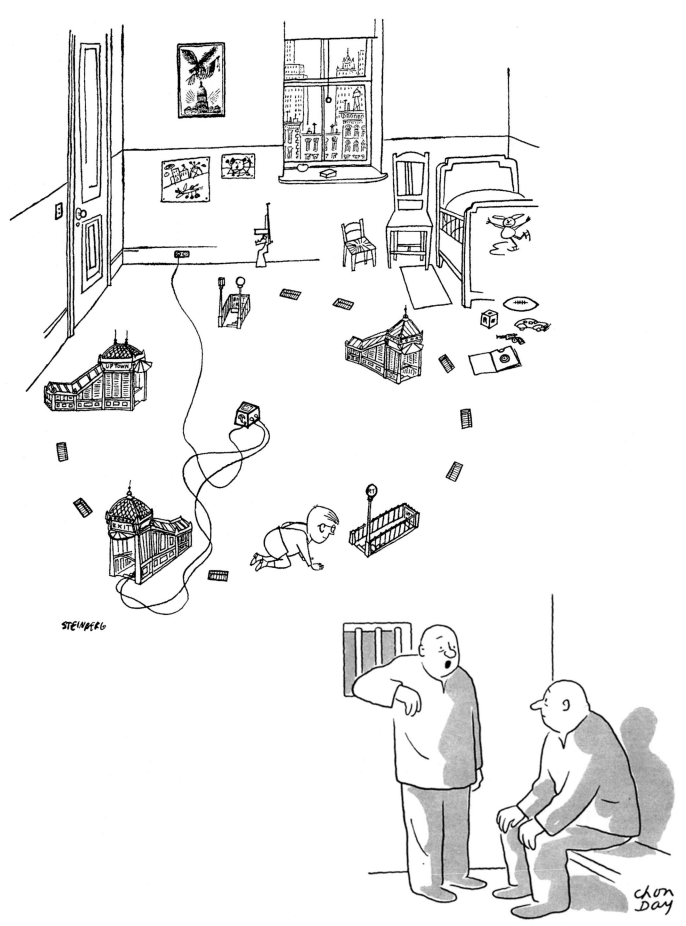

"My big regret is that I didn't start earlier.
I'da been out by now."

"I like your looks, Ramsey. You're hired."

"Oh, darling, can you step out for a moment?"

"Macy's is closed!"

"There! How do *you* like being splashed?"

"Goodness, Murray, it wouldn't be a picnic without ants."

1949

1

"Fill 'er up."

"In football, sonny, you're supposed to throw it back."

4   5   6   7

"With you, it's different. You've got talent,
courage, imagination, savoir faire. . ."

"What gets me is why they made all their
buildings look like banks."

"<u>Irma</u>, go put some clothes on!"

"Take him off 'Atom Man,' 'Torture Comics,' and 'Superman,' and put him on Peter Rabbit, Mickey Mouse, and Downey Duckling for a while."

"My God! That's Mount Powell over there!"

"Harold! You promised!"

"Say, Joe, what does a North Korean look like?"

"Now, this complete, all-in-one model has a thirty-nine-tube television receiver, equipped for both black-and-white and color reception; AM and FM radio; a record-player geared for 33 1/3 r.p.m., 45 r.p.m., and 78 r.p.m.; automatic record-changer; the latest thing in a wire recorder; and this large, roomy cabinet at the bottom, in case anything new is invented."

"We must have made a wrong turn somewhere."

"You are charged with disorderly conduct, indecent exposure, and impersonating an officer."

"Look at it this way, Conroy—the longer they stay out, the longer you're a free man."

*"Look who wants to spend Saturday
afternoon with his daddy!"*

*"Well, at least they aren't sitting back waiting for
a handout from the government."*

"Marge, is it yellow or gray you look like hell in?"

"And now we present 'Mary and Bill,' the story of a family that
might be your next-door neighbors, and of their everyday life
among everyday people just like yourselves . . ."

"Suppose he doesn't get the best marks in his class.
Do you get the highest salary in your office?"

"They'd make a cute couple, except for her."

"What burns me up is that the answer is right here somewhere, staring us in the face."

"Come and get me!"

"What would you suggest for somebody who wants a mink coat?"

NUDITY

In *New Yorker* cartoons of the nineteen-twenties, there was plenty of female nudity: on posters, in burlesque shows, in the doctor's office. In an Otto Soglow series of 1928, a hypnotist forces a woman to strip, but doesn't quite have full control over her—in the final panel, she sticks her tongue out at him. The cartoons with nudity weren't generally the sexiest cartoons, either; William Crawford Galbraith's drawings were suggestive and sensual, but his characters generally kept their clothes on. (Nudist colonies, a fad of the thirties, inspired their own separate sub-genre, including a puckish Soglow drawing in which a nude man passes a nude woman and, through force of habit, turns his head to glance at her departing form.) After the Second World War, the presentation of the female nude continued to evolve. And if Whitney Darrow, Jr.,'s cartoon showing a woman in a laundromat waiting for her clothes was distinctly unglamorous, and Richard Taylor's offended sunbather somewhat oblivious, other cartoons compensated with a more evident erotic agenda. This was thanks largely to Sam Cobean, who was a master of mental undressing. Cobean, who drew more than three hundred cartoons between 1944 and 1952, explored every possible permutation of the phenomenon: a man on a traffic island imagines the woman next to him naked on a desert island; a man imagines a fellow-pedestrian as an attractive nude until she snubs him, at which point he imagines her as an unattractive nude; and, perhaps offering the definition of an optimist, a man looks at the half-man, half-woman in a circus freak show and pictures only the female half undressed.

"I want to report a helicopter."

1951

"And they provide a good deal of insulation, of course."

"Oh, Mrs. Williamson!"

"If <u>I'm</u> stupid, what about you? You married me, didn't you?"

"It's all right. I just tripped on the last step."

"It isn't the Ds and Fs that bother me. It's that A for effort."

"Hold it! He's been reprieved!"

"See, Grouchy? We haven't missed a thing—the score is still nothing to nothing."

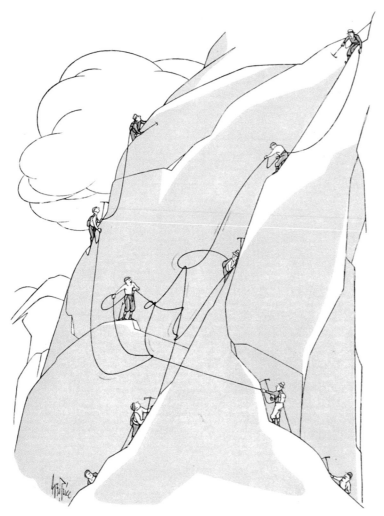

"Next time maybe you guys will watch where the hell you're going!"

"It's hard to imagine what people used to do before television, isn't it?"

1 2 3 4 5 6

"Whatever do you see in poor little me?"

"Please don't go to any trouble. We can only stay a minute."

1951

"This is the time of year when you begin to appreciate the 'Times's' fuller coverage."

"Hold it, Grace. There's someone pulling out now."

"Why, _I_ could do that!"

"Good heavens, Emma! I thought _this_ was you."

"Quite an upset. He's losing to everybody!"

1

2

1952

"I hate to mention it, but you've got his coat buttoned the wrong way. "

"I always feel like a damn fool when I'm down to my last one."

"Girls go for a fellow with money. For quick cash, men, visit the nearest office of the Friendly Loan Company."

"But, gosh, Daddy likes this program, and, after all, Melvin, it only happens once every four years."

"All right, now, a little smile."

1952

cobean

"You're absolutely right, sir. And now that you've won a free
trip to Chile, would you care to try for return passage?"

"Just the kind of day that makes you feel good to be alive!"

"*Enrich the soil with humus, which can be obtained from any nearby bog. . .*"

"<u>*Please!*</u> *There happens to be a lady present.*"

"It isn't often one sees a bowler these days."

"*That's just an expression, Mrs. Brown, I don't really want to take him home with me.*"

"It's the children, darling—back from camp."

Charles Addams, internationally famous for his ghoulish creation the Addams Family, was one of the sunniest souls ever to grace *The New Yorker's* offices. He drew effortlessly, drank freely, and enjoyed the company of glamorous women. (He married three of them.)

In fact, Addams's work was always more surreal than macabre. King Kong imprisoned in a glass skyscraper; identical twins, with identical inventions, reunited at the patent office; and, of course, the skier whose tracks diverge around a tree. The response was often a shiver but never a scream.

The first cartoons that Addams sold to the magazine, in the early thirties, were executed in simple pen outline. He quickly mastered a sophisticated wash-based technique, however, and began to produce drawings whose elegance rivalled that of Garrett Price's and Richard Decker's. But to his peers, notably Saul Steinberg, it was the subtle intelligence behind the work that mattered. Addams, unlike most cartoonists of the time, who relied on gag writers, came up with his own ideas; only Thurber, Steig, and Steinberg were as successful at fusing concept and style.

Like many artists, Addams was a collector. His passions were medieval armor and vintage cars. He died peacefully, in 1988, at the wheel of one of his favorite roadsters, parked in front of his Manhattan apartment building.

In the course of half a century, Addams contributed more than a thousand cartoons to *The New Yorker*. In a memorial tribute, the magazine's editor, William Shawn (who, notoriously, stopped running cartoons of the Addams family once they appeared on television), wrote, "*The New Yorker* was not complete until Addams joined it."

"Congratulations! It's a baby."

"I'm sorry, sonny. We've run out of candy."

1953

"Speak up! Speak up! How do you expect
me to hear you?"

"It's Oglub's boat all right, but
it doesn't look like Oglub."

"Death ray, fiddlesticks! Why, it doesn't even slow them up."

"Saw a robin today."

1953

"I'm anemic."

"I backed up last time."

"They _all_ are. That's what he's in for."

"You're fired!"

"When we used to listen to the radio,
what were we looking at?"

1953

"That's the man! I'd know him anywhere."

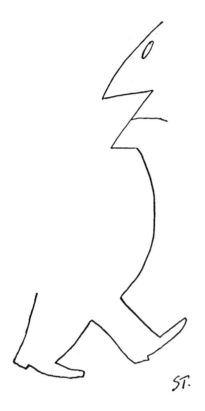

"*I played on Notre Dame.*"

1953

"My, you do have a green thumb!"

"I'm afraid we owe you an apology."

"I give up, Robert. What does have two horns, one eye, and creeps?"

"Martha, I can't find a damned thing!"

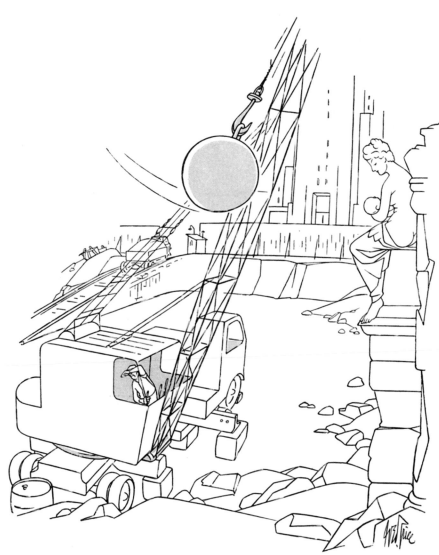

1954

"By this time the audience is with her."

"Lord, what a day!"

"I swore they'd never take me alive, but when the time came I figured what the hell."

"No, no, Bill! You're a commissioner now."

"Aunt Claire asked you a question, dear.
Are you the pitcher or the catcher?"

"My God! Didn't anybody *tell* them?"

"Which hand?"

"It's not a fit night out for man nor beast."

"Did it ever occur to you how you look to *them*?"

"Say, I think I see where we went off. Isn't eight times seven fifty-six?"

"I do think, Dr. Wurdle, that what we are witnessing here is an example of what might well be called ecological coördination."

"I hope they have to do a retake. This cherry cobbler is delicious."

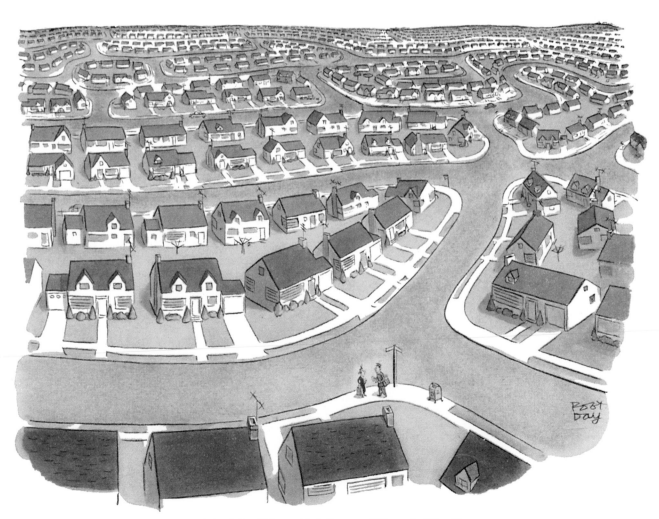

"I'm Mrs. Edward M. Barnes. Where do I live?"

Most of the early *New Yorker* cartoons about television plowed a fairly narrow furrow of humor that commented upon the ability of the new invention to disrupt (or mirror) the reality of its viewers. Sam Cobean imagines a woman, just out of the shower, covering herself up because of a man on the television screen; a similar plight befalls Richard Taylor's adulterous couple; and Chon Day's dog, home alone, licks the only human face in sight. Slowly, though, jokes shift away from the ontological nature of the medium and toward a broader social context: televisions in homes, but just as often in bars, as in Anatol Kovarsky's 1948 cartoon in which each group of patrons has a television. By the early fifties, jokes about television start to seem more like today's. In 1952—the first year the national political conventions were televised—Robert J. Day comments on the preposterousness of on-air election-day analysis.

"My God! My husband!"

"Here's the first return—from upstate. Two districts reporting out of a total of ten thousand three hundred and forty-eight. Seventy-two for Eisenhower, sixty-seven for Stevenson. Mr. Bayes, would you care to analyze the trend as you see it up to this point?"

THE FOURTH DECADE
1955-1964

THE FOURTH DECADE
1955-1964

JOHN UPDIKE

"I don't know what my father does all day. All I know is it makes him sick at his stomach."

"Please hurry, Hilary. Your soup's getting dirty."

The decade 1955-64 did not think of itself as a halcyon time, but in retrospect it seems so. Between the Korean police action and the Vietnam involvement, it was the Cold War in its purest form, as a show of global threats and feints, brinkmanship brought to a terrifying but casualty-free climax in the Cuban missile crisis of 1962. The vast Communist world and embattled capitalism somehow agreed to avoid a third World War, while in America consumerism and industrial production struck a balance that produced, for the masses, a greater ease of living. As one caption has it, "You know how it is. You have a little more, you live a little better."

The suburbs were the arena of the new plenty, at the expense of cities and farms. Not that the men in gray flannel suits were altogether happy. There were stirrings, even under the anodyne Eisenhower. In popular culture, early rock drowned out the mellow remnants of the big-band era; in painting, the stern and heroic canvases of Abstract Expressionism morphed into the cheerful junk art of Pop and the deadpan quiddity of Minimalism; in writing, baroque mandarins such as Bellow and Nabokov added new, lighter notes to the sonorities of our native naturalism. A certain lightness and gaiety, indeed, permeated the décor and the mindset of a hardworking land.

The microcosm of *New Yorker* cartoons reflects the cultural macrocosm spottily, with a time lag. The foremost domestic issue of the time was the struggle of the black minority for civil rights, yet people of color are almost totally absent from these cartoons, except for a joke showing an anxious drugstore clerk facing a diverse mob of customers and calling out, "Joe, these people say they want flesh-colored Band-Aids." This joke, in fact, was no joke, as the Johnson & Johnson marketers have discovered. Though Peter Arno's sculpturally solid brushstrokes and exclamatory visages still appeared in this decade, his world of tuxedoed elderly rich and impossibly busty and wide-eyed nymphs (who never think of bringing sexual-harassment charges) belonged to a bygone era of metropolitan stylization. So, too, Syd Hoff's plump tenement dwellers, in their slips and sleeveless undershirts, and George Price's hatchet-faced dwellers in decaying, lovingly detailed interiors furnished entirely, it appears, with hasty purchases at garage sales. These lively types represented old economic divisions and old apportionments of the national esprit. One graphic artist of genius, Charles Saxon, emerged to depict, in unfailingly beautiful and dashing charcoal renderings, *Homo suburbianis*—middle-aged, modestly prosperous, suffering somewhat the same civilized discontents as Thurber's less dapper, less auto-conscious citizens of the two previous decades.

Harold Ross had died abruptly in 1951, and the presence of the more introspective William Shawn at the helm is reflected in the deepening intellectual adventuring of Saul Steinberg and William Steig into, respectively, the philosophy and the psychology of the Zeitgeist. Both men pushed *The New Yorker*'s envelope into new, profounder, captionless realms of cartooning. In the meantime, there was topical news. Cars grew fins; space travel by terrestrials and extraterrestrials grabbed the imagination. A Luddite revolt against the computer, still in a massive box, was envisioned. The razing of Penn Station and the erection of the Guggenheim Museum were noted. Anatol Kovarsky and others reached across the millennia toward ancient worlds, where Trojan horses treacherously loomed and an Egyptian slave hauling rocks for the Pyramids claimed, "It's an honor to be associated with an enterprise of this magnitude."

The magnitude of free-world leadership weighed on the collective mind: "The Russians have the Intercontinental Ballistic Missile, and we have the Edsel." There was the nagging threat of nuclear war ("Do you hear something ticking?") and the global ingratitude of the less fortunate: as embassy windows crash, huddled diplomats observe, "It's ironical. Our Peace Corps built their brickyard." At home, feminine dissent rears up: a well-heeled woman asks her scowling, cigar-chomping mate, "Darling, would it upset you terribly if I came out for peace?" The daughters of the bourgeoisie don sandals and black pants and let their hair grow long, occasioning one matron to sniff to another, "Thank God *I'm* not an individual." In an elegant Saxon cartoon five months later, a well-padded matron says to another, of a young woman who has come to a cocktail party in a poncho, "They sent her to Bennington to lose her southern accent, and then she turned her back on *everything*." Toward the end of 1964, a salesman gives an ominous pitch to a customer: "This toy is designed to hasten the child's adjustment to the world around him. No matter how carefully he puts it together, it won't work."

"This toy is designed to hasten the child's adjustment to the world around him. No matter how carefully he puts it together, it won't work."

"They sent her to Bennington to lose her Southern accent, and then she turned her back on everything."

"Do you hear something ticking?"

"Somehow I miss feeling that pride of ownership a Cadillac owner should have."

"There! A message of good will for all mankind."

"I'm sure your feelings do you credit, Mrs. Carter,
but you must dust this along with the others."

"On second thought, I think I'll have the vegetable plate."

243

"Shakespeare's got the right idea.
People just want to be entertained."

"I wonder if he could take me next. I think mine's contagious."

"I know, Sarge. There's nothing you can tell me that I haven't already told myself."

"Will somebody please adjust that damn blind?"

"Collapse, Smith!"

"Go ahead, ask him something."

"Either cheer up or take off the hat."

"So what if people do laugh? The world can use a little more laughter, can't it?"

"Looks like Wesselman's hit on something interesting."

"You're right—it _doesn't_ have a blade!"

"That's *you*, I suppose."

"I'm sorry, Madam. That's all the places there are."

"This is the hour I love best, when they're all tucked away and sound
asleep and I'm kind of like a shepherd watching over them all."

"By George, I think you're right!"

"Why, that's Prescott! Suppose he knows something we don't know?"

1956

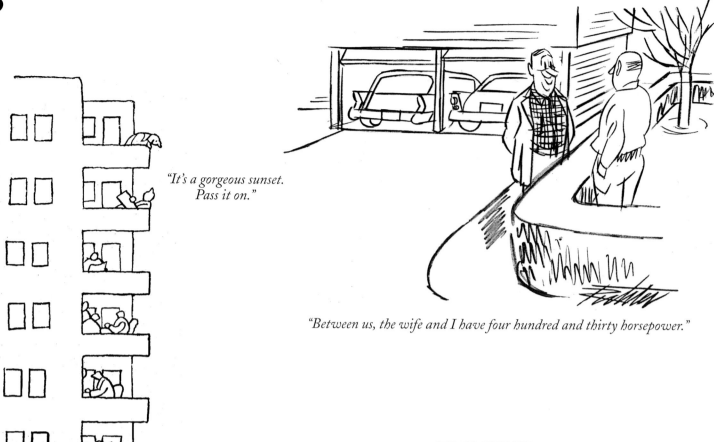

"It's a gorgeous sunset.
Pass it on."

"Between us, the wife and I have four hundred and thirty horsepower."

"Seems like an awful lot of cellar for a one-family house."

"See that little knob on the top left? Turn that to 50. Now look at the ring
on the front—the one with the green line on it. Turn that so the line points to f 11.
Now look at the next ring—it's got a little red line. Turn that to . . ."

"It is I."

"Can't you get along with _anybody_?"

"Just a minute, there—you with the
relieved look. Come back here!"

"Oh, I beg your pardon! I thought you were extinct."

"I had a little drink about an hour ago . . ."

"Let's figure ninety for rent. Telephone, electricity, and gas, twenty.
Food, sixty-five. Laundry, cleaning, say another twenty . . ."

1956

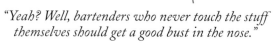
"Yeah? Well, bartenders who never touch the stuff themselves should get a good bust in the nose."

"You never looked at _me_ that way!"

"This is a hell of a way to run a railroad!
You call that a dry Martini?"

"Oh, and one thing more, Joe. Would you see that my subscriptions to
'Time,' 'Life,' and 'Collier's' are discontinued until further notice?"

WILLIAM STEIG

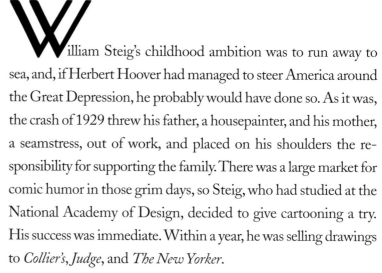

W illiam Steig's childhood ambition was to run away to sea, and, if Herbert Hoover had managed to steer America around the Great Depression, he probably would have done so. As it was, the crash of 1929 threw his father, a housepainter, and his mother, a seamstress, out of work, and placed on his shoulders the responsibility for supporting the family. There was a large market for comic humor in those grim days, so Steig, who had studied at the National Academy of Design, decided to give cartooning a try. His success was immediate. Within a year, he was selling drawings to *Collier's*, *Judge*, and *The New Yorker*.

Steig's earliest work drew on his memories of friends and neighbors in the tenements of the Bronx. The "Small Fry" series, introduced in 1932, was based on his boyhood adventures with his pals in the Orion Athletic Club. By the mid-thirties, Steig's star was rising rapidly at *The New Yorker*, but his success lagged behind his ambitions. In a 1937 interview, he expressed impatience with the standard gag-cartoon format and a desire to move beyond it. In fact, he already had.

Steig began turning out "symbolic drawings," pictures and words in which he ruminated on the individual's endless struggle to be freed from the iron bonds of social conformity. This was heavy stuff—too heavy, in fact, for Harold Ross's lighthearted weekly. As was the case with James Thurber, *The New Yorker* was embarrassingly slow to recognize the value of the unfamiliar work. Steig, undeterred, began publishing the drawings in books such as "About People" (1939), "The Lonely Ones" (1942), and "All Embarrassed" (1948). Perhaps the magazine just needed time to catch up; at any rate, by the mid-fifties Steig's more idiosyncratic work, like Steinberg's, sat comfortably in the magazine's pages alongside more traditional drawings by Darrow, Mischa Richter, and George Price.

Steig remained a prolific and revered contributor of drawings, spreads, and glorious covers to *The New Yorker* until his death, in 2003. He also wrote and illustrated children's books, including "Sylvester and the Magic Pebble" (a Caldecott Award winner) and "Shrek!" (which became an animated film). Although his impact on other artists was liberating and profound, he had no successors. As Maurice Sendak once said, "There is no school of Bill Steig. There is only Bill Steig."

"Up betimes and crowed."

The New Suit

"Now neither of you has it."

The Burden of Self-Consciousness

257

1957

"Well, what sort of a lousy day did you have today?"

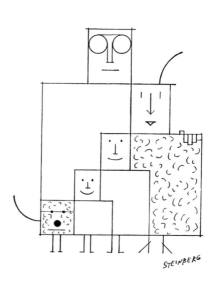

"May I see the script again, Miss Dolan?"

"What was the name of that tranquillizer we took?"

1957

"But if it's Tuesday, it has to be Siena."

"You sure know how to pick 'em. Mine keeps peeling all over the place."

"Surely, Son, you can find something to paint indoors."

"We could never have done it without him."

"Well, it was sort of like a cookout."

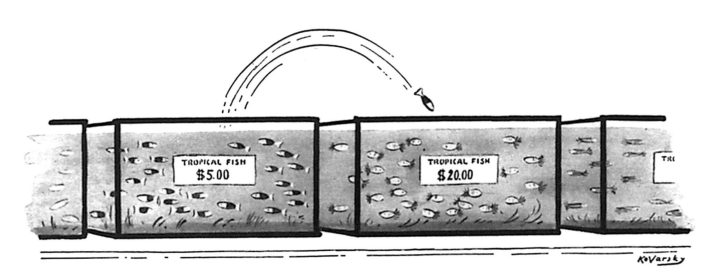

1957

*"Pop, tell me again how jazz came up
the river from New Orleans."*

"But after Ed Sullivan, then what?"

"To hell with a balanced portfolio. I want you to sell my Fenwick Chemical and sell it now."

"Do you think I like being a hypochondriac?"

"I roamed the world trying to find myself, and then I came home and
discovered happiness right here in my own back yard."

"But let's not forget the roadwork, shall we?"

"Which country is the least mad at us?"

"And the Haves, you might say, are divided
into the Gives and Give Nots."

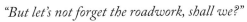

"Stop saying I'll live to be ninety. I *am* ninety."

1958

"The United States Embassy? Just follow us.
We're on our way there right now."

"Hold your hat! Here we go!"

"No, I found my ball. I'm looking for the golf course."

"Don't just stand there, lady!
Call the Hundred-and-Thirty-first
Airborne Infantry."

"Don't worry. If it turns out tobacco is harmful, we can always quit."

"This is a diplomatic mission of the utmost delicacy. The question is,
who's the best man for it—John Foster Dulles or Satchmo?"

267

"Mr. Kenney will be delayed for a few minutes, but he wants
you to go ahead and start thinking without him."

"X, IX, VIII, VII, VI, V, IV, III. . ."

"If we lose this district by just two votes, God help you!"

"Do you call C-minus catching up with the Russians?"

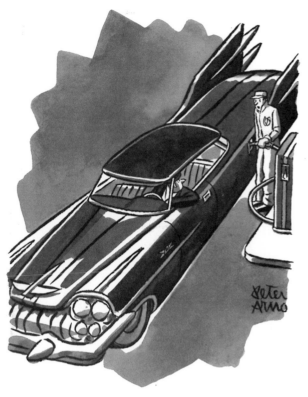

"Would you mind turning your motor off, sir?
You're gaining on me."

"I'm sicker than they realize."

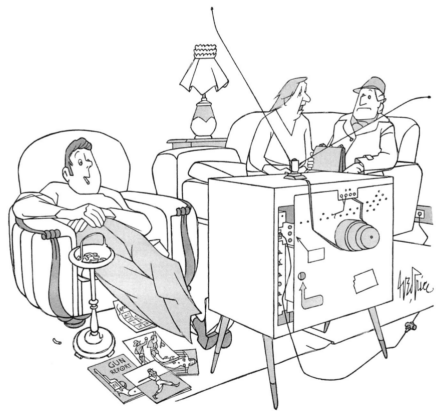

"Success came too early. When he was ten, he hit three homers in three times up
in the Little League, and nothing has seemed worthwhile since."

1958

"I am not the kind of man who indulges in lavish promises about the future. But I make so bold as to say this—that had I been in office over the past two years this great nation of ours would have been the first to launch a sputnik, there would have been no troubles in Iraq and Lebanon to inflame the Middle East, there . . ."

"I ask you, gentlemen, is that the face of a dishonest man?"

"Henry!"

"I thought I heard a twig snap."

"Are they allowed to do that on Fifth Avenue?"

"We're in Japanese waters, that's for sure."

"You'll find everything here, Comrade—your American passport, Social Security number, birth certificate, driver's license, and Diners' Club card."

"See if you can pass that car. He would have wanted it that way."

"Oh, there you are! Goodness, for a minute I thought your briefcase came home without you!"

"Communism is when the leader goes on the wagon, the whole damn country goes on the wagon."

273

"Well, at last!"

"Lily is the child. Violet is the dog."

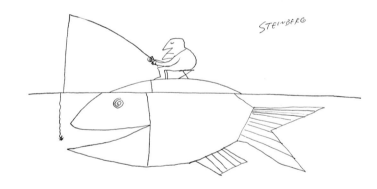

1.

F.B.I. REPORTS JUVENILE
CRIME ON INCREASE

2.

FARMER GOES BERSERK
KILLS TWO IN-LAWS,
SIX CHILDREN

3.

BERLIN THREAT GROWS

"Oh, stop complaining! It's an honor to be associated with an enterprise of this magnitude."

"You're darn right I'm a Puritan!"

4.

TREASURY AGENTS TO
CRACK DOWN

5.

FALLOUT SHELTERS
CLAIMED VITAL
TO SURVIVAL

6.

"It could be worse. He could be out chasing you know what."

"*I'm the captain of this ship!*"

"*Be patient, Madam. The judging of the funny hats will resume as soon as we get ashore.*"

"Don't forget to compliment him on his green thumb."

"It looks great to me. Let's run it up the flagpole and see if anyone salutes."

"Will you please stop bothering us, Comrade? You'll read it in 'Izvestia' when we surpass America."

"No, no, no! Thirty days hath September!"

"I understand that in your country this thing is done quite differently."

"Why is it, Oogluck, that though the years may come and the years may go, you still never fail to find it amusing when someone slips and falls on the ice?"

"This is she."

"So the putt is worth eight thousand dollars to him.
What's your cut? Ten per cent?"

"Oh, I give him full credit for inventing fire,
but what's he done since?"

"This is ridiculous. Why couldn't we meet them downstream?"

"Look, dear, the world!"

"Believe me, for myself money means nothing. But as the custodian of my genius I must demand these prices."

"OF COURSE, IT IS CONVENIENT TO THE AIRPORT!"

STEINBERG

"Pointless rebellion against authority, if you ask me."

"Look, Buster, I'm trying to get some shut-eye."

"Give us three or four more years, and then 'Watch out, America!'"

1960

THE DAY THE TRAINS STOPPED

William Archibald knew it was to be a day different from all the others. A cuff-button was missing from his shirt; the Times hadn't been delivered; and the clocks had stopped during the night, owing to a power failure. Archibald said to his wife, Gloria, "I'll bet the damned trains won't run, either."

On the branch line, forty-seven people gathered between 7:47 and 10:39. When the fifth scheduled train failed to appear, Fred Fitzdyke, a commuter since 1945, said, "When I started using this line, they ran it like clockwork."

Edward R. Myers stood at the spot on the platform where the first car always stopped. His feeling of well-being, the result of having arrived five minutes early and parking in a good spot, began to dissipate. "Why doesn't somebody do something about this?" he thought. "Nobody gets mad anymore."

Osgood Maddux thought that the trains had simply been permanently discontinued. But he was always thinking that the oil burner was leaking, or that he heard prowlers fiddling with the Mercedes in the garage, so he didn't say anything.

George Ward telephoned his assistant, Donald Chapman, at the office, and told him he didn't know when he would be able to get to the shop. "You'll have to carry the ball," he said to Chapman, who told him to go home and take it easy.

Ralph Miller, Ronald Smith, Gene Clifford, and Henry Thompson adjourned to the station luncheonette, where they played bridge until four o'clock in the afternoon.

Arthur Fenster was close to, but not actually a part of, a conversation between John Amster, Dick Burnside, Jr., and Tom Stanley, all golfers and members of the Chipowee Country Club. They were discussing their game. Fenster hoped they might start talking about the delay, so he could say something casual, like "You'd think they could make some sort of announcement. It wouldn't cost them anything."

Baggagemaster Fred Folsom answered all questions by saying nobody told him anything, he didn't know anything, and he didn't know anybody who did know anything.

Mrs. Lewis Fisher, member of the Republican Town Committee, said to her neighbor, Mrs. Lloyd Lefcourt, "There's more to this than meets the eye." Mrs. Lefcourt, who had matinée tickets to "The Sound of Music," said, "Be that as it may, discourtesy is certainly the order of the day."

At twelve o'clock noon, it became clear to Willis Palmer that the trains were not going to arrive. That, in fact, there never again would be an 8:47 to Grand Central. He thought of his family, in the neat board-and-batten split-level on the hill— of Francine, his wife; and Bill and Debby, his two young children. He knew he would have to give up his job in New York and try to find something in the country. Something close to home. Palmer folded his "Herald Tribune" neatly, dropped it in a litter basket, and walked slowly toward his Plymouth station wagon.

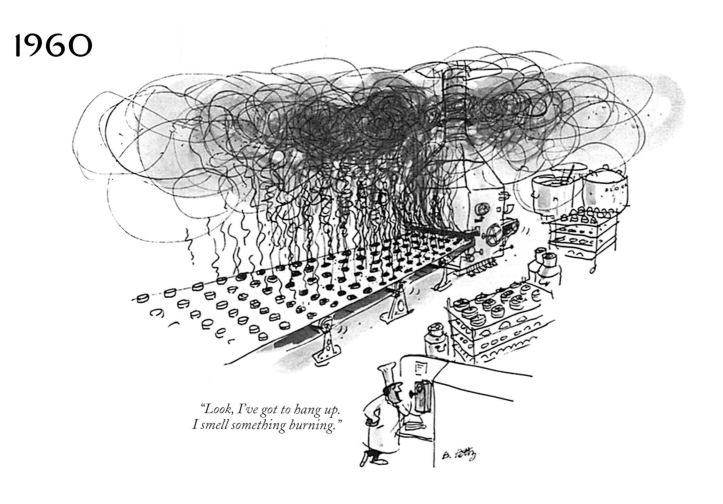

"Look, I've got to hang up.
I smell something burning."

"They don't build them the way they used to!"

"My advice to you is to eat, drink, and be merry."

"You seem troubled, Brother Timothy. Is anything worrying you? I mean besides the sins of the world, the vanities of mankind, and that sort of thing."

1961

"O.K., so you're forty, you've lived half of your life.
Look at the bright side. If you were a horse,
you'd already be dead fifteen years."

"The President and Jackie you know. Then there's Joe,
the father, and Rose, the mother. And then Bob and Ethel,
Ted and Joan, Eunice and Sarge, and then . . ."

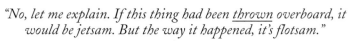

"No, let me explain. If this thing had been <u>thrown</u> overboard, it would be jetsam. But the way it happened, it's flotsam."

"What makes you think Frank Sinatra, Dean Martin, and all that bunch are so happy?"

"Wait, Son. I've got a better idea."

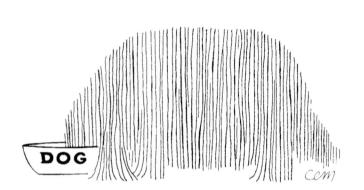

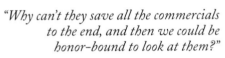

"Why can't they save all the commercials to the end, and then we could be honor-bound to look at them?"

"Aeschylus is good, I suppose, but I go to the theatre to relax."

"I'm waiting."

"Oh, I don't know. Every night you got to remember to turn the damn thing on, every morning you got to remember to turn the damn thing off, and every six months you got to remember to change the damn bulb."

"His spatter is masterful, but his
dribbles lack conviction."

"Yeah, it's handy, but I still say the old challenge is gone."

"I don't know. Lately, everything looks like Jackie Kennedy to me."

"Harrison J. Endicott speaking."

"When you drive, I lock up. When I drive, you lock up. Right?"

"Oh, for goodness' sake! Smoke!"

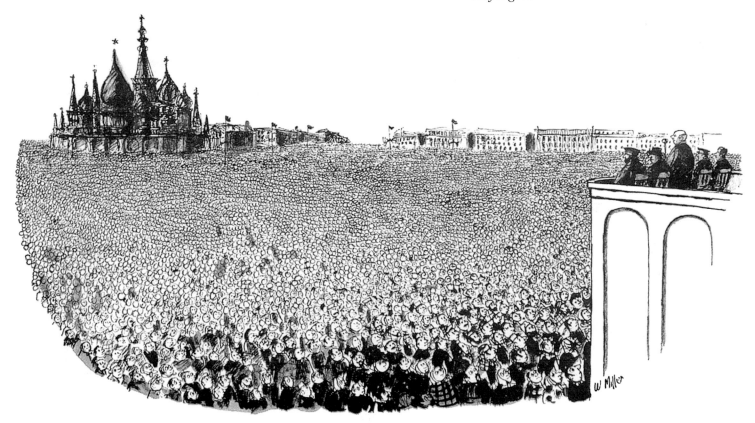

"You're probably wondering why we asked you here today."

1962

"O.K. with you if I look at it in the dawn's early light?"

"Ah, here's your guide now!"

"Why, it's Daphne—home from Foxcroft."

"You think you're so damn Cordon Bleu!"

"Thank God I'm not an individual!"

"How often have you asked yourself, 'What can I do to fight Communism?' Well, sir, you can fight Communism by making capitalism work, and you can make capitalism work by buying this new model."

"Well, either he's a giant or we're awfully tiny."

"Now let's talk about you."

"I realize that those of you who are planning to
go into psychiatry may find this dull."

"Shouldn't there be only nine of us up here?"

299

"Count them again. There *can't* be more trouble
spots than there are countries."

"Just a minute, young man. That's not quite the way
we do things here at the Ford Foundation."

"Love to stay, but we have a sitter."

"Suddenly, I have a dreadful urge to be merry."

*"Darling, would it upset you terribly
if I came out for peace?"*

CARS

The fifties and sixties were the era of the interstate highway, the commuter suburb, and the car—and, with ever-longer bodies and bigger engines, American automobiles were an easy target for *New Yorker* cartoonists, both visually and thematically. In 1956, Garrett Price drew a garage door that could not close because of a pair of telltale fins; a William O'Brian cartoon from the next year shows off maximalist engineering at its finest. Cars and driving were also a natural subject for sequence cartoons—a series of panels, usually without a caption, that combined aspects of the Keystone Kops and Eadweard Muybridge. But automotive humor was, in another way, like golf humor or money humor: many of the jokes that purported to be about cars were really about women. Witness a Barney Tobey drawing from the mid-fifties, depicting two women standing next to their car, which has crashed into a tree. Tobey and others returned again and again to the notion that women didn't understand how cars (or male drivers) worked and so wreaked havoc whenever and wherever they ventured on the road.

"I hope it didn't do anything to the horsepower. Fred's so proud of that."

*"Ronald, you know that little maple out front,
the one you said ought to be taken out . . ."*

"Power to spare! They can say that again!"

1963

"All right, Wilenski. Go in there and make me tear up this suicide note."

W Miller

"He may be a fine veterinarian, but we're going to get some funny looks."

"Ah, the curse is beginning to work!"

"Philip has a marvellous tax man.
He's just the teeniest bit crooked."

"Someone must love someone very much indeed."

"Where do you want Penn Station?"

"Why do you have to be the only one to say he's uncomfortable?"

"Now listen, Murphy! You've paid your debt to society, so get out of here!"

"Once I've said hello, I don't know what else to say."

"I'm sure it's all right. It's a _horse_ you have to worry about."

"I've forgotten. Which Louis am I?"

"As I understand it, then, your credo is that
everything is a lot of malarkey."

"Well, no wonder! You forgot to yell 'Timber!'"

1963

"Joe, these people say they want flesh-colored Band-Aids."

"She should have done that twenty years ago."

"Look! Jim has the ball! See him run! Run, Jim, run!"

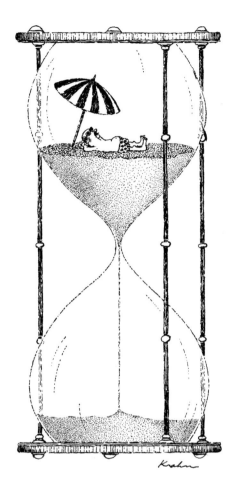

"Your contributions to the fund for the new wing to the High Priests' Tabernacle have been gratefully received. The Passion Fruit Festival was well attended, and we thank those Virgins who gave of their time to make it a success. Keep up the good work, Virgins. For the young marrieds there will be a meeting at the volcano's edge at the next full moon."

"It seems ridiculous to get rid of it now, with Christmas only a couple of months away."

"Sergeant, I hardly know where to begin."

"I know what I am, but I can't pronounce it."

"Because it's here, that's why."

"The thing is, sir, are you referring to your status quo or _my_ status quo?"

"And I say you're spoiling him."

311

"Lindsay, you're picturing my old loves again!"

"I will not talk to myself, I will not talk to myself."

"Herb reads 'Fortune' and 'Sports Illustrated,' and I read 'Time'
and 'Life.' That way we get the over-all picture."

"Just once I wish we could go somewhere without the children!"

"You're a damn sore loser, Lee."

"Jane, I promise. I'll be a good daddy."

"Then what happened?"

"Suppose we start by skipping the Acropolis."

"He's a good artist, but he obviously has nothing to say."

"Excuse me, excuse me, excuse me, excuse me, excuse, me..."

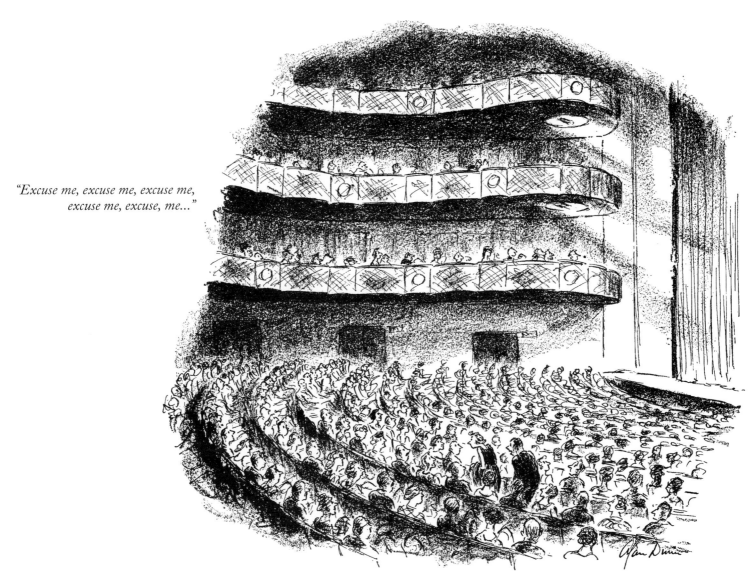

"And I thoroughly understand the problems of the caveman, because I'm a caveman myself."

"Face it, baby. You don't know the warp from the woof."

"... It is a pleasant accompaniment to fish, shellfish, and the lighter meats, but its delicate flavor is perhaps even more appreciated at the end of the meal with melon or dessert."

"Marcia, you must come. We're having a few friends in for group therapy."

1964

"What do you mean, we've got to be
running along? We live here."

"The ball, I presume, is me."

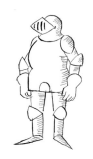    

"Help! I'm being held prisoner!"

CHRYSLER BUILDING AT 42ND STREET

The art critic Harold Rosenberg once described Saul Steinberg as "a writer of pictures, an architect of speech and sounds, and a draftsman of philosophical reflections." Had this high-flown praise preceded Steinberg's arrival at *The New Yorker*, the editor, Harold Ross (a supreme pragmatist), would surely have slammed the door in his face. Fortunately, the accolades began appearing only after the artist was well established at the magazine.

Steinberg was born in Romania in 1914. He moved to Italy in the thirties to study architecture, and in the early days of the Second World War he fled to America. (Not without some difficulties: he was turned away at Ellis Island, and only later, after landing in Santo Domingo and mailing some drawings to *The New Yorker*, did he get a visa, with Ross's help.) He worked for Army intelligence during the war, and some of his first work for *The New Yorker* was graphic reportage from his postings in India, China, and North Africa. It was not until after the war that Steinberg's concept of drawing as a way of reasoning on paper began to emerge.

His chosen subject was America, which he examined with the critical but passionate eye of an anthropologist. As he sifted through the familiar icons of our culture—Uncle Sam, Santa Claus, Mickey Mouse—Steinberg gradually developed his unique visual syntax. The Chrysler Building was his favorite amalgam of art and commerce, and in its shadow the streets were always crowded with punks, whores, and crocodiles who roamed like harmless dogs.

Although Steinberg's influence on his contemporaries was enormous, his greatest legacy was, most likely, not to other artists but to his audience. He offered them a rare gift: a new way of looking at themselves and their world (including, of course, his archetypal New Yorker's view of the world).

Steinberg died in 1999, but his unpublished work has continued to appear in the magazine—proving that, sixty years after his first drawings appeared, his ability to delight and instruct remains undiminished.

Radicals question Marx.

STEINBERG

STEINBERG

THE FIFTH DECADE
1965-1974

THE FIFTH DECADE
1965-1974

CALVIN TRILLIN

"I feel like a damn fool."

"Of course, what I'd really like to do is direct."

I think of the years between 1965 and 1975 as the period when I was trying desperately to get at least one of my cartoon ideas into *The New Yorker*, but I can understand that some historians would describe it differently. A lot of them would presumably refer to this period as "the sixties." You could argue that the first Southern lunch-counter sit-in, on February 1, 1960, begat the Mississippi Freedom Summer of 1964, which begat the Berkeley Free Speech Movement, which begat much else; for most of the country, though, the fifties lingered well into the next decade. Members of the Class of 1967 at, say, Princeton were, for the most part, people who looked and thought not much differently from their older brothers in the Class of 1958 or, for that matter, from their fathers in the Class of 1932. The shake-up of American society that came to be known as "the sixties" took place in the late sixties and early seventies—coincidentally, around the time I'd been at *The New Yorker* long enough to feel comfortable about pestering its artists with cartoon ideas in the elevator.

I wish I could say that the cartoons I suggested were about challenges to one sort of authority or another, but, truth be told, I specialized in animal cartoons. The first one I can remember suggesting—it was when one of the artists made the mistake of lingering a bit too long at the water cooler—was set in a children's zoo where kids line up to feed cuddly animals. A little girl who has finally reached the head of the line is holding out some lettuce to a rabbit, and the rabbit is saying, "Thanks awfully. It's delicious, but I couldn't eat another bite."

"Animals don't talk in *New Yorker* cartoons," I was told by the artist I'd cornered. Animals, of course, talk in *The New Yorker* all the time. I suppose he simply considered this a kinder response than "That is the dumbest idea I've ever heard."

My problem was not that I was out of touch with the times. *New Yorker* cartoons of this period rarely reflected the turmoil symbolized by events like Woodstock or the March on the Pentagon. Those that did tended to picture a conventional middle-aged person responding without much enthusiasm to the unconventional behavior of a young person—from a mother making wry comments on her son's musical taste to an updated version of that unreconstructed couple Peter Arno pictured in the thirties saying to two other couples, "Come along. We're going to the Trans-Lux to hiss Roosevelt."

Cartoonists in 1967, like cartoonists in 1958 or even 1932, were interested in human relationships that are not greatly affected by particulars of the world around them. Often, the cartoonists returned to the themes that cartoonists have used since the magazine's earliest days, in the way Hollywood directors have always used the Old West—the mad scientist, the visitors from outer space, the sensible wife deflating her stuffy or pretentious or silly husband, the desert island, the man arriving at the Pearly Gates, the defendant in front of the judge, and, of course, talking animals.

I couldn't even score with non-talking animals. Once during that period, I approached a cartoonist with what I thought was a boffo idea: An overweight woman in a riding costume is patting a horse on the nose the way people do when they offer a cube of sugar, but she's offering artificial sweetener instead.

"It would be hard to draw the label on the sweetener so people could read it," he said.

"It wouldn't be hard for someone who didn't have fat fingers," I said.

Yes, the thought that I might never get a cartoon into *The New Yorker* might have made me a bit testy. Then, in the spring of 1975, I returned from working on a story in Charleston, South Carolina—a city that had long been engrossed in the sort of architectural preservation that most of the rest of the country was just beginning to take an interest in. (A couple of years later, I did a piece about New England shopping areas called "Thoughts Brought On by Prolonged Exposure to Exposed Brick.") I was at the water cooler again, telling a few loiterers about having come across in Charleston what I thought was a pile of bricks and rubble. Then I'd spotted a small sign in front of the pile: "Another historic Charleston house awaiting restoration."

As we went on to discuss the glories of Charleston she-crab soup, a cartoonist in the water-cooler crowd put his finger up in the gesture the mad scientist in *New Yorker* cartoons sometimes uses when about to say "Eureka!" Then he marched off to his office. A couple of weeks later, the cartoon I hadn't realized I was suggesting appeared in the magazine. Does that count?

*"Harry, take it from me. You're doing
yourself more harm than good."*

1965

"The way I see it, they give us a quarter, and we swing wide the gates of a great metropolis."

"Why can't those people leave peace to the experts?"

"Yes, I can remember when it was nothing but
forest land as far as you could see."

"Hi! I'm Greg Holbrook, born in L.A., now
live in Stamford with my wife and three kids, went to
school at Exeter, graduated Yale '38, did a two-year
hitch in the Navy, now write copy for McCann-
Erickson, my hobbies are tennis and sailing.
Who are you and what do you do?"

"I said, 'Get off'!"

1965

"Anything else, Ma'am? Check your oil? Test your battery?
Rob? Cheat? Lie? Kill?"

"What we don't understand is why you can't
stay _in_ Princeton and think things out."

"Seventeen major European cities in twenty-one days."

"He's a brilliant attorney, but he can't stand to lose a case."

"So much for kinetic art, eh, Leo?"

"Good grief, Marge! Not my pajamas, too!"

1965

"Feels good, though, doesn't it?"

"Well, enough about me. What sort of a day did you have?"

"You remembered!"

"Poor Jackson! He had to dance that little jig."

"But does it ever get that cold?"

331

"For a kindly old man, he's mighty quick with the whip."

"Let's just step outside and test the creditability of your deterrent."

"Oh, no! I erased last time!"

"Stop digging, Professor! You've reached the
mandatory retirement age!"

"Make a sharp left, then two rights, then another sharp left . . ."

"But, sir, many analysts consider this only a long-overdue correctional movement, following which the market will resume its upward course, with a rally expected to penetrate previous Dow-Jones highs by the year's end."

"Say bye-bye."

"I'm making a spot check, sir. Does your
room have a Gideon?"

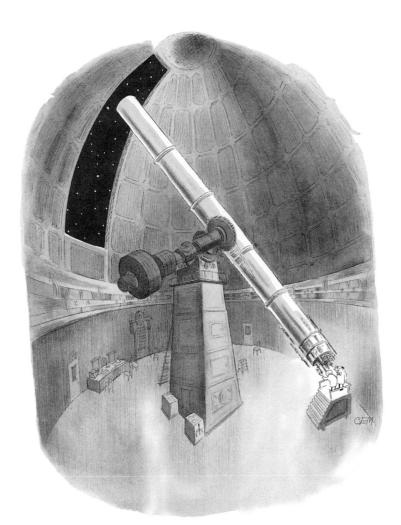

"What I like is the way they twinkle."

"April 20: The weather continues sunny and warm."

"I happen to know Ralph Nader's mother drives this model."

"Sometimes I wonder if we haven't carried ecumenism a bit too far."

"It's not advertising anything, damn it!"

STOP THE WAR IN VIETNAM

"Don't look at me!"

"Never!"

*"I know sex is no longer a taboo subject. I just don't feel
like discussing it all the time, that's all."*

"Have they no shame?"

"Because this is where the action
is going to be, baby."

"It's publish or perish, and he hasn't published."

"Oh dear, the bell! We have to go back."

"The Master Ramachandra is on vacation.
Concentrate on your breathing, meditate,
pay your dues. This is a recording."

"You just can't talk to that bunch. They all avoided probate."

"Moping is not relaxing!"

"Dear Aunt Frieda: Thank you very much for the large book . . ."

"It's nice, dear, but shouldn't you have asked Daddy, since it's his car?"

*"This is your dad, Son. Your mother and I think it's time
you stopped collecting degrees and came home."*

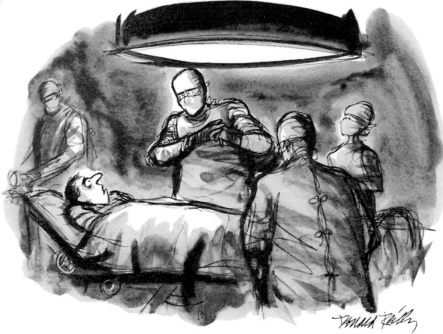

"Wait a minute! How do I know you're not George Plimpton?"

"I slept there once."

"It seems to me the winters are colder than they used to be."

"I don't think I ever before realized the distinct difference
between northern and southern California."

"Hello! What's this?"

"Hobson! How can you think of
food at a time like this?"

"You look great."

"I did my job, I grabbed my pile, and yet no voice
at eventide has cried 'Well done!'"

"They don't look like wives."

"If you're so good, why can't you ever strike
twice in the same place?"

"What's it say, Margaret?
I'm still not used to these bifocals."

THE SPACE PROGRAM

"I can remember when this was all craters."

In a speech to Congress in May of 1961, President John F. Kennedy vowed that the United States would have a man on the moon by the end of the decade. He didn't mention that the nation would also have several dozen cartoons about the space program; that went without saying. In March of 1965, Bruce Petty imagined a fanciful training center in which astronauts did calisthenics and lifted weights; later that same year, Rowland B. Wilson showed a group of scientists trying to reconcile astrophysics and astrology, and Stan Hunt placed a discussion about humanity's manifest destiny where it belonged—in a bar. Many of the images dealt directly with anxiety about what, or whom, we would find in space. A Lee Lorenz panel from October of 1965 portrayed some remarkably hospitable aliens, while those in Edward Frascino's 1966 Martian press conference lament, "The planet Earth, with unprovoked belligerence, has landed troops on her moon." In the months before the moon landing, on July 20, 1969, speculation ran rampant in the magazine's pages. But artists had been in space long before the scientists got there, and, by the time Armstrong and Aldrin stepped out of their capsule, cartoonists had decided that the subject was a little too familiar: witness Lee Lorenz's scene of a rapt father and his jaded son.

"Gee whizz, Pop, we've seen this before!"

"Why, they're just plain folks, like us!"

"As long as there was a Sea of Tranquillity anywhere in the universe, you can be damned sure that sooner or later man would slam–bang something right in the middle of it."

"On the other hand, if we launch after the twenty-first, Neptune will be dominant in the twelfth house, with Capricorn on the ascendant."

"*Give us this day no sonic boom.*"

"Oh, stop worrying about humanity's problems!
Let humanity worry about its own problems!"

"Miss Peters, would you type this searing blast at the honkie
power structure in triplicate for me, please?"

"But, Walter, what if _everybody_ felt an
obligation to his or her conscience?"

"Nancy!"

"*Mini, midi, maxi. Maxi, midi, mini . . .*"

"*That's the Hudson River School, son.*"

"Aren't you being a little arrogant, son? Here's Lieutenant Colonel Farrington, Major Stark, Captain Truelove, Lieutenant Castle, and myself, all older and more experienced than you, and we think the war is very moral."

"Oh, for Pete's sake, lady! Go ahead and touch it."

"I did it! I did it! I found a
substitute for quality!"

"How many times must I tell you? Stoop!"

"These steps are killing me. I say we settle out of court."

"Well, there she goes—the 5:08 to Los Angeles. Right on time!"

"Ariadne! How many times have I told you not to bring home those ugly, crummy, corny toys you get when you visit your Daddy?"

"The third from the corner, I understand, was designed by a famous architect."

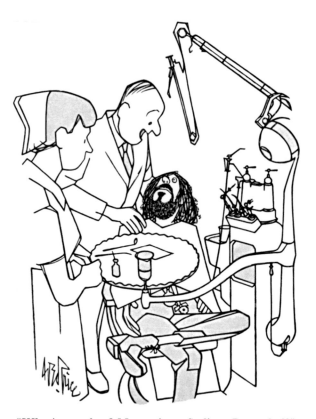

"What's your bag? Novocain or Sodium Pentothal?"

"I suppose we have Helen Gurley Brown to thank for this."

"By the way, some of us have begun to feel that 'Because it's there' is not reason enough."

U.S. CUSTOMS

"You sure give up easy."

355

"*Same old ice, same old aurora borealis, same old everything!*"

"*There's no denying the profound impact all this has on the course of human life, but let's never forget one thing. It's still love that makes the world go round.*"

"For want of a better word, I call my idea 'taxes.'
And here's the way it works."

"I think it's a crime to spend billions going
to the moon when repertory theatre in this
country is more dead than alive."

357

" 'Cogito, ergo sum' is all very well for you, but what about me?"

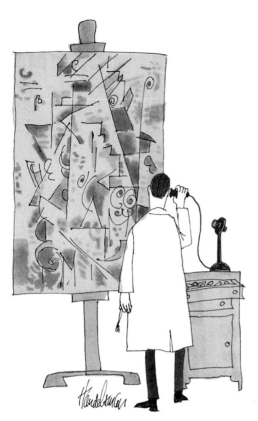

*"Hello, Braque? Picasso here.
Cubism is out."*

Dear Shirley—
    I HATE you. Here are my reasons.

"Where do you stash the porno, Cookie?"

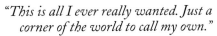
"This is all I ever really wanted. Just a corner of the world to call my own."

"Miss Peterson, may I go home? I can't assimilate any more data today."

"You can't change human nature."

"Quick! Get your gun, Pa! Here come the suburbs."

"Of course it's a beautiful job, dear, and the detail is exquisite, but don't you think it's a trifle busy?"

"Well, speaking as one who has been out of the swim for some time . . ."

"Go down there and make them laugh."

1969

B. Petty

"Princeton, did you say? How interesting.
I'm a Yale man myself."

"What would you do if you had a million dollars—tax free, I mean?"

"Visiting hours are over, Mrs. Glenhorn."

"I've heard that outside of working hours he's really a rather decent sort."

"Do we have any anti–Christmas cards?"

"There's really not much to tell. I just grew up and married the girl next door."

"I have this recurring dream about reclining on a bed of wild rice."

"Liberals!"

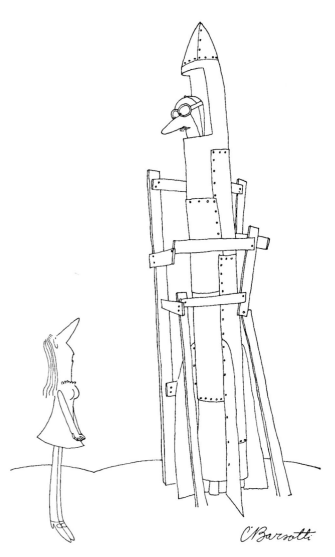

"But, Father, is running away ever an answer?"

"I am a bird of paradise, and, needless to say, I am lost."

"Celeste, I admit I'm not fit to breathe the same air."

"He's charged with expressing contempt for data-processing."

"I do ballet, conservation, starvation, cancer research, the needy,
a little art, and a smidgen for Farmington."

"Buzz off, Louise! That was only till death us did part."

"I couldn't disagree with you more. I think _yours_ is greener."

"If political ferment bugs you, you might be happier
with our All-Dictatorship Cruise Itinerary."

"What's so great about due process?
Due process got me ten years."

"Oh! Trompe-l'oeil."

"I don't see that our situation is especially improved."

"You know, the idea of taxation with representation doesn't appeal to me very much, either."

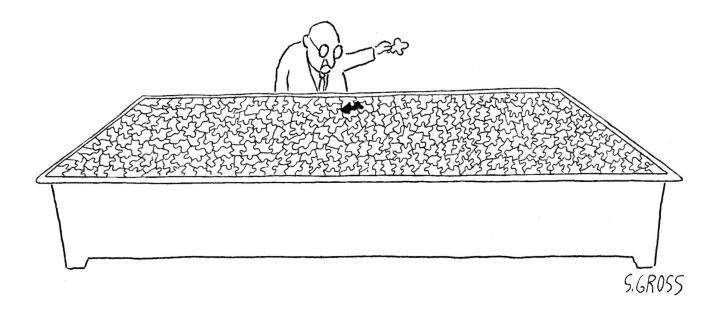

S.GROSS

"So *that's* where it goes! Well, I'd like to thank you fellows for bringing this to my attention."

"He didn't really die of anything. He was a hypochondriac."

"We younger fleas demand a bigger say in the running of this dog."

369

"I'm afraid you'll have to be more specific, Ma'am."

"Not another change of venue, Counsellor!"

"Be patient. When your time comes, we'll call you."

"We're here to escape religious persecution.
What are you here for?"

"Getting much flak from Women's Lib?"

"My goodness, this _is_ a surprise! I didn't know that you people skied!"

"There are plenty of jobs around. People just don't want to work."

"Arthur, there's a thing at the door says it's escaped from
M.I.T. and can we please plug it in for the night."

"I grant your point, but not because I agree
with you. I'm under sedation."

"It's good to know, Colonel Snively, that there's one small
part of Africa that will be forever England."

"I used to think it was wrong to coddle criminals, but that was before I became a criminal."

"Now look what you've done!"

"Certainly I'm proud to be an Eskimo! That doesn't mean I enjoy freezing my tail off."

"Have you told your readers about _me_? About how I
walked into your life when all your friends and family
had turned their backs on you? And about how I brought
you love and hope for a brighter tomorrow?"

"I'm afraid I'm not the
Jerry Rubin you want.
However, lots of luck, power
to the pigs, and so on."

"Come to bed, Ridgely. If your boomerang were going
to return, it would have been back hours ago."

"It is we."

"If we pull this off, we've made burglary history!"

George Booth's path to *The New Yorker* was as strewn with potholes and detours as the rural back roads of his native Missouri. He drew his first cartoon, a racing car stuck in the mud, at the age of three, and had his first published in the magazine forty years later. Along the way, he spent eight years in the Marines (he was a staff cartoonist for *Leatherneck*, the Corps's official magazine) and worked freelance around New York, editing a basket of obscure trade magazines.

Rejection slips from his earliest attempts to crack the cartoon market were slowly crowding him out of his apartment when he received some encouragement from his fellow-cartoonist Charles Barsotti, in 1969. Barsotti, then the cartoon editor of *The Saturday Evening Post,* planned a four-page spread of Booth's work—scheduled, as it turned out, for the very week the *Post* folded. The editor of *The New Yorker*, William Shawn, supplied a happy ending when he plucked Booth and Barsotti from the wreckage of the *Post* and brought them aboard his magazine.

Booth quickly found an enthusiastic audience for his irate spinsters, grumpy couples, sadistic mechanics, careering cats, and, of course, the Booth dog, who has joined the Thurber men and the Addams family as a *New Yorker* icon. His drawings have been studied by Ph.D.s, printed on greeting cards, and even set to music (mixed chorus and organ)—though his best and truest accompanist is, of course, the violin-playing Mrs. Ritterhouse (who put her instrument down, in sorrow, in the only cartoon that *The New Yorker* ran the week after the September 11th attacks).

Booth is a tall, loose-jointed gentleman, soft-spoken and unfailingly polite. He laughs easily, especially at his own jokes, and likes to pass on the advice he received from his mother: "Always act like you know what you are doing. Stick to it—and give it plenty of oomph."

"Whistle, you dumb bastard!"

"That, honey, is probably an end."

"I've got an idea for a story: Gus and Ethel live on Long Island, on
the North Shore. He works sixteen hours a day writing fiction. Ethel never
goes out, never does anything except fix Gus sandwiches, and in the end
she becomes a nympho-lesbo-killer-whore. Here's your sandwich."

1972

"After all these years, you still feel guilt?
You should be ashamed of yourself."

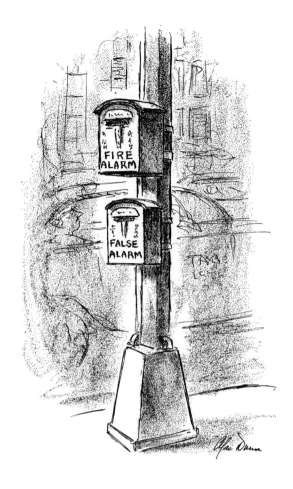

"And this, gentlemen, is Mr. Quodley, my immediate inferior."

"But gosh, Ursula, together we'd be exactly what
every major advertiser is trying to reach."

VIVE LE ROI

"The air I breathe is filthy, my food is poisoned, my automobile is a gas-guzzling behemoth, my school taxes have doubled, the Internal Revenue Service plans to take the fillings out of my teeth, my wife is fifty-three and pregnant, my dog bit a lawyer's kid, my son steals, my mother-in-law is a Communist, my daughter ran off with a fink, and now you tell me that if I don't back up and let you have the right-of-way I'll be in trouble."

1972

"This is a complete retrospective."

"I'm fifty-seven years old, but with the wind-chill factor I feel eighty-three."

"Say, we pandas _are_ cute!"

"Is that Miss Ms or Mrs. Ms?"

"I'll tell you what it is. It's two hundred thousand peasants from permissive peasant homes, that's what it is."

"It's hard to believe that someday _we'll_ be just so much nostalgia."

"My God! Webbed Feet!"

"Maybe a little shrubbery or something would help."

"Your friend is more than welcome, dear, but we just want you to know that your father and I didn't do anything funny till after we were married."

"Hot as all getout, isn't it?"

1972

"Steer clear of that one. *Every day is always the first day of the rest of his life.*"

"No offense intended, José. We were only wondering why you never dress like the rest of us gauchos."

"If it turns me on, it's smut."

"That banquet was most delicious, and yet now, somehow,
once again I feel the pang of hunger."

"I wonder, sir, if you would indulge me in a rather unusual request?"

"We'll have to keep your car another day. There's a deviled egg in the carburetor."

"Charles, I've had it with you and your goddam moods."

"No, Dad, I don't wan't to toss the old pill around."

"Now, Charles, tell me all about
the black experience."

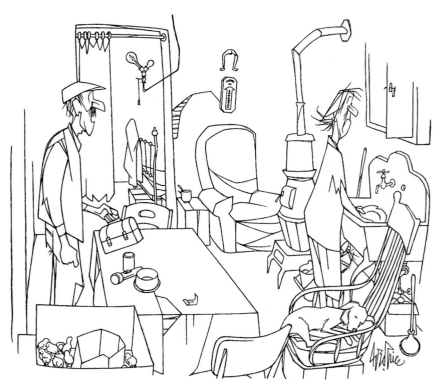

"I keep having this recurring nightmare that I've gone out and bought a three-piece suit."

"I heard a bit of good news today. We shall pass this way but once."

"'Not the real you'? Well, of course it's not the real you. The real you is bald."

1973

"My boy, Grand-pere is not the one to ask about such things.
I have lived eighty-seven peaceful and happy years in Montoire-sur-le-Loire
without the past anterior verb form."

"For God's sake! Pick up your <u>own</u> damn money!"

"Mr. Prentice is *not* your father. Alex Binster is *not* your brother. The anxiety you feel is not genuine. Dr. Froclich will return from vacation September 15th. Hang on."

"Oh, may I freshen your drink, Dr. Marshall?"

"It's a love story. Nobody's ahead."

S. GROSS

- ALICE & JEREMY -

"We've had our ups and downs, Jeremy, but over all it's been a good marriage."

DON'T BLAME ME! I NEVER VOTED IN MY LIFE

D. Fradon

HOW TO BE YOUR OWN BEST FRIEND

W. Miller

"Listen, Momma, don't wait up. I'm with this nice boy, and we're having a
bite at Zum Zum. We're going to catch the show at the Music Hall, and on
the way home we'll probably pop into a Baskin-Robbins for a cone."

"I'm afraid, Son, this will never be yours. I'm having myself cloned."

"Brooks Brothers? Arthur T. Stargis here.
I believe a mistake has been made."

"The blahs are here."

"I'd just like to know what in hell is
happening, that's all! I'd like to know
what in hell is happening! Do you
know what in hell is happening?"

"It seems some days like I make a little progress, then other days it seems like I'm not getting anywhere at all."

UNAUTHORIZED
PERSONNEL
ONLY

"Sweetie, Aaron has written a little poem about the energy crisis."

1974

S.GROSS

"There's the pressure from my public, naturally, as well as the pressure from my publisher, my agent, and all that. But the real pressure comes from that devil inside that makes me different from other men, that makes me a writer. But, of course, you know all about pressure, grinding out those papers at Sarah Lawrence."

"Congratulations, keep moving, please. Congratulations, keep moving, please. Congratulations . . ."

". . . and your view is undisturbed by the only eyesore in this lovely village."

"Hello? Beasts of the Field? This is Lou, over in Birds of the Air. Anything funny going on over at your end?"

"Religious freedom is my immediate goal, but my long-range plan is to go into real estate."

" 'Ignorance of the law is no excuse.' Golly! I never heard that one! Did you ever hear that one?"

"Let's face it, Tom. A society that's paying its
Frank Sinatras and Johnny Carsons more than
its yous and mes is out of whack."

"Is there someone else, Narcissus?"

"I've called the family together to announce that, because of
inflation, I'm going to have to let two of you go."

"The January issue comes out in October, the April issue comes out in January, the July issue comes out in April, and the October issue comes out in July, but I don't have any of them."

"I used to be a management consultant, but now I'm into making up songs and poems."

"Grayson is a liberal in social matters, a conservative in economic matters, and a homicidal psychopath in political matters."

*"Do you ever have one of those days when
everything seems un-Constitutional?"*

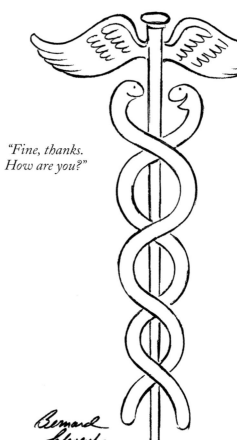

*"Fine, thanks.
How are you?"*

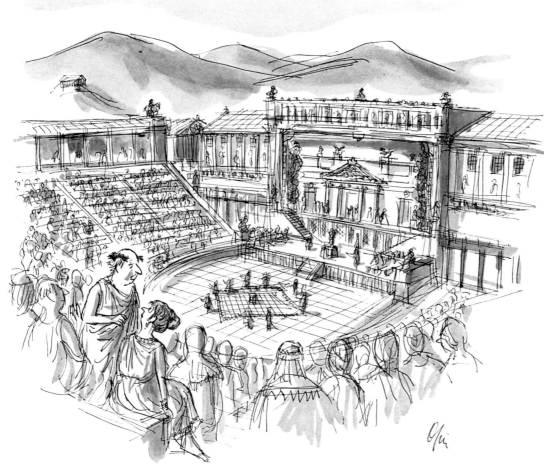

"Let's skip the epilogue and beat the crowd."

"But I digress."

"At this point, the product smiles and says,
'Good day, Mr. Froggie.'"

*"Oh dear! I've got all the husbands and wives separated,
but I forgot about you live-togethers."*

THE SIXTH DECADE
1975-1984

THE *SIXTH* DECADE
1975-1984

IAN FRAZIER

"Is it too cutesy?"

"Senior Vice-President Buffington reporting, sir. Requests permission to advance and be recognized."

Recently, I was watching a baseball game on TV with some friends who were born in Russia. Play had stopped while the manager and the team trainer came to the mound to examine a blister on the pitcher's throwing hand. The men peered at the hurt finger with expressions of deep seriousness. One of my friends asked why pitchers didn't wear gloves on their throwing hands to protect from such injuries. It was a question that would never have crossed the mind of anyone who grew up watching the game. Throwing a baseball so a batter can't hit it is an act of strength plus delicacy and cunning that can be accomplished successfully only by the bare hand. In our machine-run world, such acts seem to be getting rarer. An outstanding few, however, remain.

Drawing a cartoon is among them. You can't do it with a gloved hand or with a robot hand, no matter how well designed. You need your plain human hand, a pen or something like a pen, and a shimmer of inspiration approaching grace. The gift is one of the greatest that humans have. When I was a kid, I thought tossing off a drawing that made people laugh or say "Wow!" was about as cool as striking out Ted Williams on three pitches. Guys at school would draw in their notebooks and pass them around to be admired. Some had certain drawings they specialized in: one guy did elaborate race cars, another did Woody Woodpecker; a lot of guys could draw rifles, tanks, bloody bayonets, and Army men. I had outdoor fantasies, so I drew fishing equipment—fly rods, mostly. And, probably because my parents were lifelong subscribers and worshipful readers of *The New Yorker*, I drew images I had traced from the magazine's cartoons. My signature drawing was a man in a tie and blazer at a cocktail party with his left hand in his pants pocket and his right hand holding a glass. I do not remember that the drawing was much of a success with the guys at study hall.

I have a theory, supported only by my opinion, that many or most cartoons in general used to possess a strong element of "guy to guy." I think this came about because of the First and Second World Wars. During the war, soldiers did cartoons and drawings and passed them around for amusement or other reasons. As they went across Europe in '44 and '45, they drew the "Kilroy Was Here" peeking-over-the-fence character on walls. Naturally, a lot of their drawings were of sexy-looking women. Afterward, in peacetime, that guy-to-guy spirit became a part of cartoons in *The New Yorker* and elsewhere. In the years between and after the wars, you had a lot of cartoons in which one of the participants was a wide-eyed doll named Miss Buxbaum or Miss Hunniford or Miss Knightly. Generic caption: "May I speak to you in private for a moment, Miss Rimpkins?"

In the years we're considering, the mid-seventies to the mid-eighties, the guy-to-guy element (in *New Yorker* cartoons, anyway) began to fade. There are probably social and cultural reasons for this, but my powers of analysis are exhausted. In the seventies and after, cartoons came less from one specific group's shared assumptions and more from out of nowhere. A good example is Jack Ziegler's "The Empire State Building and a Side of Fries," which depicts the two objects side by side, just as the caption says. Another example is T. K. Atherton's drawing of a "Desk-Top Organizer" that includes spaces for feather boa, chocolate sprinkles, right elbow, left elbow, and pieces of eight. Another is Roz Chast's "Little Things," the first drawing she published in *The New Yorker*. The Little Things, which seem somehow familiar while being completely unidentifiable, are labelled with names like "chent," "tiv," and "kellat." Here, clearly, a whole new species of cartoon had emerged.

Humor involves moment and perspective—"you had to be there"—both of which change a little every day and a lot over a decade or three. But you don't have to "get" a cartoon to like it. I pored over *New Yorker* cartoons before I knew anything about cocktail parties or Miss Buxbaum or New York City. And though I think I more or less "get" the humor in (for example) George Booth's "Ip Gissa Gul"—another cartoon whose publication I remember as a semi-historic event—I find that I can look and re-look at that cartoon and others long after the joke has registered. I study the chin-tucked-in posture of the "well-bred, well-read, and well-fed" people in a William Hamilton cartoon, or any number of wacky objects in George Price drawings—the way he drew the back of a television set in one of his domestic scenes sometimes outdid the entire rest of the issue for eloquence—or the fuzzy, old-hippie droop of an Ed Koren couple, or the expanse of a Bob Weber cityscape or a Lee Lorenz big-shot's office. The list, of course, goes on.

A cartoon is a remark made by hand and eye instead of breath. It's like a significant glance or an expressive shrug that doesn't vanish in an instant but remains its original spontaneous self indefinitely. The more you examine it, the better you see its live, black-on-white drawn lines vibrating forever like just-plucked strings.

THE EMPIRE STATE BUILDING AND A SIDE OF FRIES

"What is it this time? My maleness? My Anglo-Saxonness? My Princetonness? My lawyerness?"

"Can you help me? I want to be a normal person again."

"It was a very bleak period in my life, Louie.
Martinis didn't help. Religion didn't help. Psychiatry
didn't help. Transcendental meditation didn't help.
Yoga didn't help. But Martinis helped a little."

"It's finally happened, Mr. Cramer. 'They' are here to see you."

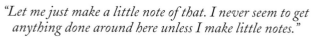

"Let me just make a little note of that. I never seem to get anything done around here unless I make little notes."

"Please! Destroy him utterly!"

"We deal with it by talking about it."

"Oh, yes, we know them. We hate them."

"Frankly, I hate weekends. They break my momentum."

"Well. That's more like it!"

"Darling, let's get divorced."

"You blow a billion here, you blow a billion there. It adds up."

"It _was_ nice. Hard times give everyone such a sense of camaraderie."

411

"My wife and I have an understanding."

"Hey, I'm thirsty. I need a drink. A drink and a liverwurst sandwich. Hey, how about a sandwich and a beer down at Gallagher's, and then we can go shoot some pool? Or maybe take in a movie. Hey, I'm talking to you."

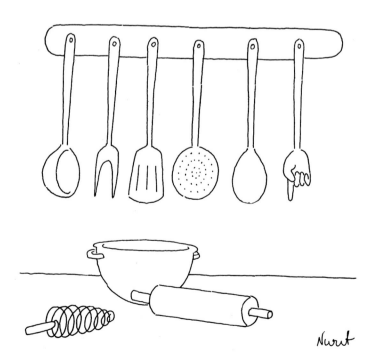

"I can't put it into layman's language for you.
I don't know any layman's language."

"Really, Karl! Can't I mention the high price of
kohlrabi without getting a manifesto?"

"*People of North Dakota! Or possibly South Dakota!*"

"*Don't panic. I'm just a sore throat.*"

"*Instead of calling me Grandpa, why don't you just call me Herb?*"

1976

"When I fell in love with you, suddenly your eyes didn't seem close together. Now they seem close together again."

"Why, Hennings, I had no idea."

"Write about dogs!"

"Why, this is fit for me!"

"Foursquare and several beers ago …

*our fatheads brought froth
upon this continent—"*

*"Found them, sir!
Your reading glasses."*

NEITHER LETHARGY, INDIFFERENCE, NOR THE GENERAL COLLAPSE OF STANDARDS WILL PREVENT THESE COURIERS FROM EVENTUALLY DELIVERING SOME OF YOUR MAIL

1976

"It *is* a superb vision of America, all right, but I can't
remember which candidate projected it."

"It's a little fiftyish, but we like it."

"George Stoner is here from Terre Haute.
He and Henry are talking over old times."

"Two separate worlds, please."

1976

"Don't worry, darling. You'll happen."

"I suppose you know you're spoiling that dog."

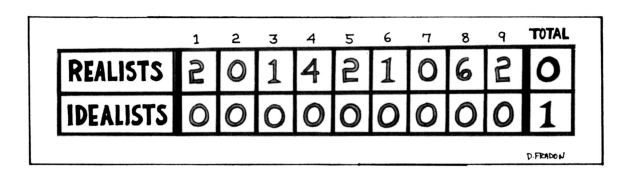

	1	2	3	4	5	6	7	8	9	TOTAL
REALISTS	2	0	1	4	2	1	0	6	2	0
IDEALISTS	0	0	0	0	0	0	0	0	0	1

D. FRADON

"It was either the knish in Coney Island, the cannoli in Little Italy, or that divinity fudge in Westchester."

"The Garbers are people who have been
through it all and survived."

SLIPPER DOGS

Some cartoon themes have been with us since the beginning of time, or at least since the beginning of *The New Yorker*—desert islands, for example, which first appeared in the early nineteen-thirties and remain a vibrant form to this day. Others enjoy a brief moment in the sun but fall out of favor when cultural mores shift, like jokes about an explorer in a pot, about to be eaten by cannibals, a setup that was popular in the forties and fifties. Then, there is the mysterious case of the slipper-bearing dog. We all know this type: the loyal four-legged friend who totes comfortable footwear to his master, who is resting in an easy chair. He's a relative of the St. Bernard with the barrel of brandy around his neck, and of the dog who brings in the newspaper. There must be dozens of cartoons from the twenties to the sixties featuring slipper-bearing hounds. But, no, there are only two: Alain's sequence of drawings from 1945, and Bruce Petty's 1964 panel, which transplants the scene to a shoe store for comic effect. After that, the motif slips out of sight. That is, until the mid-seventies, when it enjoys a baffling renaissance. Frank Modell, Mischa Richter, Chon Day, Ed Arno, and Arnie Levin all drew cartoons starring slipper dogs between 1976 and 1980. The dogs stayed on firm footing through the eighties, particularly in the work of James Stevenson, before shuffling off, once again, into relative oblivion.

SLIPPERS

"Attention, everyone! I'd like to introduce the newest member of our family."

"I used to be old, too, but it wasn't my cup of tea."

"No, you're not disturbing me, Herb.
I'm up with the chickens this morning."

THIS STRUCTURE WILL
BE TORN DOWN AND
REPLACED BY A NEW
44-STORY COOKIE

"That's Mr. Brock. He didn't have a happy
New Year, a happy Valentine's Day, a happy
St. Patrick's Day, a happy Easter, a happy Father's
Day, a happy Halloween, a happy Thanksgiving,
or a merry Christmas. He did have, however, a
safe and sane Fourth of July."

"If the New York 'Times' knows everything, it follows
that the New York 'Times' should be President."

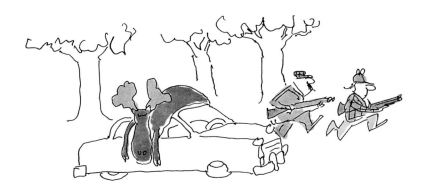

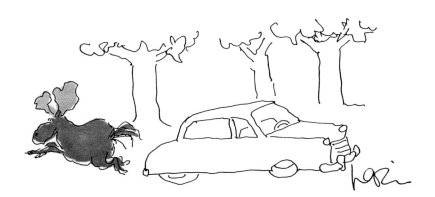

"You can't legislate morality, thank heaven."

"Let's face it, Ron. The only time we meet
each other's needs is when we fight."

427

"It's a mixed blessing."

"Meaningless statistics were up one-point-five
per cent this month over last month."

"Not the Bermuda triangle?"

SHARP PENCILS, CLEAN PAPER, GOOD LIGHT, COMFORTABLE CHAIR, HOT COFFEE, WARM ROOM...READY TO WORK...PERHAPS THE ROOM IS _TOO_ WARM...

LONG AFTER LOSING THE ELECTION, FRED GORT CONTINUED TO CAMPAIGN, THUS MAKING A MOCKERY OF THOSE REPORTERS WHO HAD LABELLED HIM "THE I-DON'T-CARE CANDIDATE."

"Now, this is Plan A. I recommend we skip it
and get right on to Plan B."

"Your duties will be simple, Wilkins—pass the bottle when
I get dry and brush away the blue-tail fly."

"I hope you don't mind. He doesn't know he's a dog."

STAR

RATS

"No, no, Miss Clark! I asked you to bring in the Mantle of Greatness, not the Cloak of Secrecy."

"One of you boys go help Mom with the groceries."

"She's not here. She's at fine stores everywhere."

"She's all work and no play."

LOTS OF IMPORTANT INFORMATION THAT YOU HAVE TO KNOW

GOSSIP, RUMORS & WACKY STUNTS

"Yes, I know, Munger. But Wallace Stevens didn't scribble his damned verses on company time."

"What a coincidence! I couldn't help noticing you're reading a book I was thinking of reading myself."

SEMI-LUXURY LINER

PIZZA PAL | BAR | O.T.B. | BAR

POOL HALL | MR. CHICKEN | BAR | PAWN SHOP

BAR | LAUNDROMAT | OLGA THE SEER | JOE'S DINER | BAR

HARDWARE | BAR | SHOP-QUIK | BAR | JIFFY DONUT SHOP | YOGI'S YOGURT

BAR | CREDIT BUREAU | NEWSSTAND | BAR | TRUCK STOP | TAKE-OUT CHINESE FOOD

BIDE-A-WEE MOTEL | THRIFT SHOP | BAR | PARKING LOT

PINBALL ALLEY

JAIL

ZIEGLER

"Actually, I'm just coming down off a kind of surprising haircut, and I think I'll just hang around the house for a while."

"Some women to see you, Anne."

S. GROSS

435

"You know, Marion, one of the things that have stood the test of time is these tassel oxfords."

"Good morning, Mrs. Kiley."

BOOTH.

S.GROSS

"I'm sorry, Travers, but I'm going to have to let you go."

"Thank God! A panel of experts!"

LIBERTY,
EQUALITY,
SORORITY

"I suppose this means the usual communiqué:
'A full and frank exchange of views.'"

"Your mom's a very special person."

"It's only the wind."

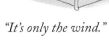

439

"Alden, which of the five senses do you value most?"

*"Look, will you forget about them? They're in the past. The
important thing is what I feel now—about you!"*

"Of course it's not my son. My son is a nitwit.
That's me, thirty years ago."

"Would you like to hear some music while you hold?"

"I'm afraid we'll have to call it quits, Irene. I love a parade."

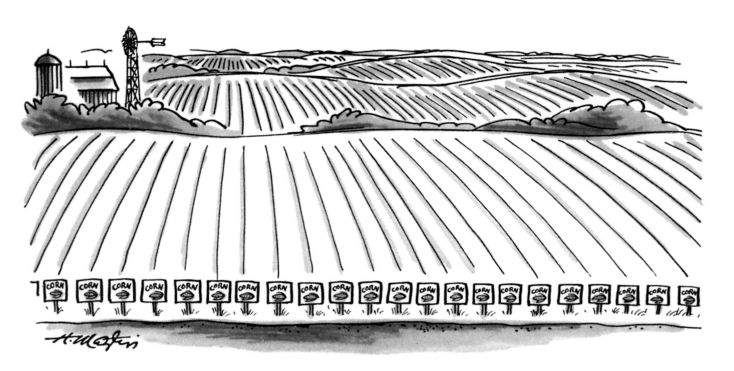

LIFE WITHOUT MOZART

"So long, Bill. This is my club. You can't come in."

WALL ST

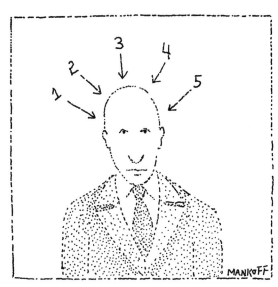

The Five Major Warning Signs of Baldness

1979

"Money is life's report card."

*"This one might be a bit out of your price range, sir.
It costs eighteen zillion dollars."*

"And what do you do to maintain your cardiovascular fitness, Miss Holt?"

"Women kiss women good night. Men kiss women good night. But men do not kiss men good night—especially in Armonk."

"Good evening, sir. As you may know, the soaring costs of recent environmental-protection legislation have forced us to pass part of this burden along to the consumer. Your share comes to $171,947.65."

"What do you do?" "I'm a lawyer."
"The law."
"I do law."
"I practice law."
"I'm an attorney."
"Something legal."

*"Would you excuse me,
Miss Arkwright? I just remembered that
I promised to forsake all others."*

"All those in favor say 'Aye.'"

"Aye."   *"Aye."*   *"Aye."*

"Aye."   *"Aye."*

"Please, Mrs. Enright, if I let you pinch-hit for Tommy, all the mothers will want to pinch-hit."

1980

THE FOUR MAJOR FOOD GROUPS

Regular:

Hamburger, cola, French fries, fruit pie.

Company:

Cracker variety, canapé, "interesting" cheese, mint.

Remorse:

Plain yogurt, soybeans, mineral water, tofu.

Silly:

Space-food sticks, gelatine mold with fruit salad in it, grasshopper pie.

R. Chast

"I'm undecided, but that doesn't mean I'm apathetic or uninformed."

"When he leaves, I'm in charge."

"Superb Martinis!"

1980

"Liverwurst is down an eighth, egg-salad is up two and a half,
and peanut-butter-and-jelly remains unchanged."

"I consider myself a passionate man, but,
of course, a lawyer first."

"Back to Square One!"

"I'm sorry, dear, but you knew I was a
bureaucrat when you married me."

"Look, everyone here loves vanilla, right? So let's start there."

TIM AND BETTY.

BETTY AND TIM.

TROUBLE AHEAD

"You're probably wondering why is this guy coming on so strong to me, right?"

"Sweetheart, could you maybe include the dog?"

"More, please. Americans overeat, and, by God, I'm an American!"

"It's not all peaches and cream, although I'll admit it is <u>mostly</u> peaches and cream."

"The service is polite and well meaning, if a little slow."

"Please forgive Edgar. He has no verbal skills."

"And don't waste your time canvassing the whole building, young man. We all think alike."

"On the other hand, we've had a lot of wonderful years in the tourist business."

"Nothing happens next. This is it."

JACK ZIEGLER

LOS ANGELES, 1928:
MICKEY MOUSE EMERGES FROM THE PRIMORDIAL OOZE

"I can't alk-tay ow-nay."

J ack Ziegler is uncomfortable with comparisons between his contribution to *The New Yorker* and those of such artists as Charles Addams, Peter Arno, and Helen Hokinson. And yet Ziegler has done just as much to shape the character of *New Yorker* cartoons. Ziegler expanded the notion of what a cartoon could be, seamlessly blending the conventions of the traditional gag panel with those of the comic strip. In doing so, he prepared the way for a new generation of comic artists, including Danny Shanahan, Arnie Levin, Robert Mankoff, and Roz Chast.

Aside from a childhood passion for comic books, there is little in Ziegler's curriculum vitae to explain his achievement: choirboy; military-high-school graduate; page boy at CBS; gofer at an ad agency. In 1972, after a short stint in the Army's language school (they taught him Russian!), Ziegler was kicking around San Francisco, recovering from a failed novel, when he decided to move back East to try his luck as a cartoonist. A boyhood friend was working at the recently launched *National Lampoon*, and they thought to collaborate on cartoons, with Ziegler drawing the pictures and his friend providing the gags. But it soon developed that Ziegler preferred to do both. Some of his first sales were to the *Lampoon*. Ziegler claims that it took him a few thousand drawings before he reached *The New Yorker:* "Five hundred before I began to get the hang of it and another thousand or two before I liked what I saw."

Today, Ziegler dispatches his work to the magazine from his studio in Las Vegas. If clues to his genius are to be found on the premises, they lie buried in files with labels such as "Foolish Behavior," "Burgers & Toast," and "Men in Trouble." Whether surreal (January 3rd at Rockefeller Center), off the wall (the gallows with the wheelchair ramp), or close to home ("Timmy, Sixth-Generation Pain in the Ass"), Ziegler's work matches his ambition: "I just try to be funny."

DISCOVERING THAT THE LIGHT AT THE END OF THE TUNNEL IS NEW JERSEY

THE DUMPLING BATHS OF SZECHWAN PROVINCE

"The following program is rated P, for 'poop.'"

457

"*I love it! It says city.*"

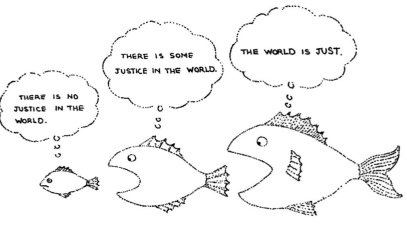

"*There's a kind of rhythm to making money that something inside me responds to.*"

"*How much would you pay for all the secrets of the universe? Wait, don't answer yet. You also get this six-quart covered combination spaghetti pot and clam steamer. Now how much would you pay?*"

The Three Certainties

DEATH

TAXES

BOBO

R. Chast

*"If it's all right with you, I thought we'd do
some long-range planning tonight."*

*"I love the Caribbean in
February!"*

BY ALLOWING THE PREDATOR TO BLEND
IN WITH HIS SURROUNDINGS, NATURE
AFFORDS HIM THE PROTECTION HE NEEDS
TO EFFECTIVELY STALK HIS PREY.

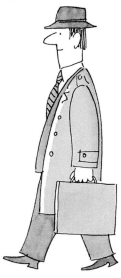

P. Steiner

"On Wall Street today, news of lower interest rates sent the stock market up, but then the expectation that these rates would be inflationary sent the market down, until the realization that lower rates might stimulate the sluggish economy pushed the market up, before it ultimately went down on fears that an overheated economy would lead to a reimposition of higher interest rates."

Separated at birth, the Mallifert twins meet accidentally.

"Most of all, I enjoy being able to work at home."

"Oh, Lord! Not another wine-and-cheese party!"

"My wife! My best friend! My favorite TV program!"

"Your car will be right down, Mr. Lundquist."

461

"Me? I'm not in a dental plan. I thought you were in a dental plan."

"... and give me good abstract-reasoning ability,
interpersonal skills, cultural perspective, linguistic
comprehension, and a high sociodynamic potential."

NEVER THE EXPERIMENT
ALWAYS THE CONTROL

"And just why do we always call my income the second income?"

"Anything wrong?"

PRISONER OF PACHELBEL

"Jesse, isn't that one of Mr. Ferguson's wheels?"

"These projected figures are a figment of our imagination. We hope you like them."

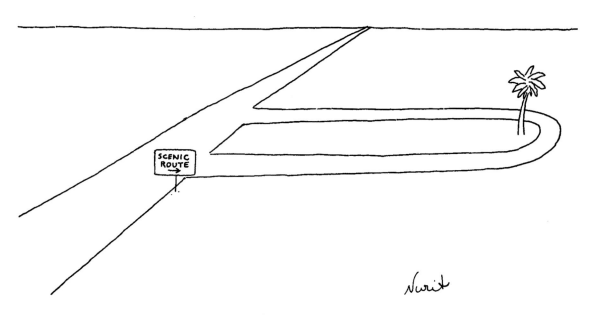

SGROSS

*"It was right where you left it—
under the table."*

PARALLEL UNIVERSES

OURS:
It's 4:27 P.M., and Mrs.N. is baking cookies.

UNIVERSE #783329860I:
It's 203:97 ZFK, and Mrs.Vvv. is baking pilkers.

UNIVERSE #80355476:
It's $\frac{109}{L}$, and Trr is baking sppooo.

UNIVERSE #$\sqrt{B}$:
It's £, and ¢ is #8✿〜 ✗∞○○.

R.Chast

"Well, so long, Bert."

MANKOFF

"It appears to be Siva, manifesting himself as Lord of Destruction, but why he's in Hartsdale on a Thursday night is beyond me."

"Good evening. I am Martha's son by a previous marriage."

"And please protect me from the appearance of wrongdoing."

"And now, for all of you out there who are in love, or if you've ever been in love, or if you think you'll be in love someday, or even if you only think you might like to be in love someday, this song is for you."

"That's just our design-team image. Our actual design team is over here."

"O.K., but change 'Her tawny body glistened beneath the azure sky'
to 'National problems demand national solutions.'"

"What's the word I want for that disposition of yours?"

"No question about it Louise—
we've been married too long."

"You know what I bet it is? I bet we're breaking up but we just don't realize it yet."

"I found the old format much more exciting."

WORKAHOLIC

1983

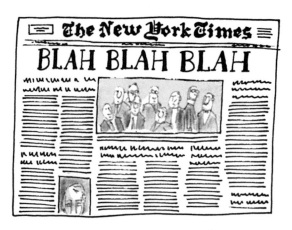

SWISS ARMY COUCH

*"What do you mean, 'Your guess is as good as mine'?
My guess is a hell of a lot __better__ than your guess!"*

HAUTE CUISINE

NOUVELLE CUISINE

CUISINE VÉRITÉ

Stuart Leeds

"How come you always take Amnesty
International's side?"

"That's the trouble with pets. They're so destructive."

"Son, you're all grown up now. You owe me two
hundred and fourteen thousand dollars."

"You may switch to the less expensive wine now."

471

1983

"I was at my sister's today. They have two pots."

"Research and development."

BEES

WORKER   QUEEN

DRONE   CONSULTANT

"Howard, I think the dog wants to go out."

THE YOUNG JACQUES COUSTEAU
AT THE BEACH
WITH HIS MOTHER

Regardez!

"But can they save themselves?"

"Maynard, I do think that just this once you should come out and see the moon!"

"Son, your mother is a remarkable woman."

"One last question, Berlinger. Is it just you, or is the whole damn Accounting Department shot full of steroids?"

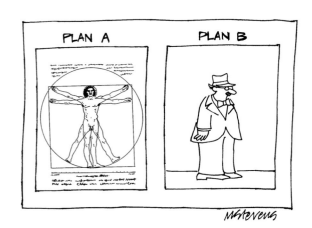

PLAN A   PLAN B

"It's good to know about trees. Just remember nobody ever made any big money knowing about trees."

"My advice is to learn all the tricks you can while you're young."

"How about that? I recently became my own person, too."

"We got it! We got the pyramid contract!"

"Front desk? There are no little candies on my pillow."

WHY THEY HAVE SPRING TRAINING

"Brockhurst has an M.B.A. from Harvard and a Ph.D. from Columbia, but everything he does is deeply rooted in the blues."

"Goodbye, Alice. I've got to get this California thing out of my system."

"The thing I like about New York, Claudia, is you."

"Sorry about this, but I just ran out of sand."

S.GROSS

"My God! I went to sleep a Democrat and I've awakened a Republican."

5 TONS

EXECUTIVE FITNESS PLAN

479

"Good God! He's giving the white-collar voters' speech to the blue collars."

"I find there's a lot of pressure to be good."

"I just realized, Howard, that everything in this apartment is more sophisticated than we are."

SUNRISE ON MOUNT HIBACHI

"Bob up and down."

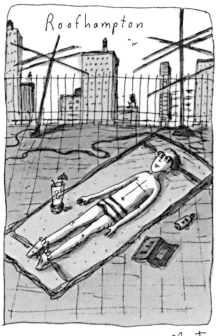

More Hamptons

Tubhampton

Fanhampton

Roofhampton

"That wasn't very nurturing of you."

"We do pretty well when you stop to think that people are basically good."

THE END OF INNOCENCE

"General Hoskins, I don't care if you are
in charge of our star-wars defense. You must
wear a regulation uniform."

"Attention, please. At 8:45 A.M. on Tuesday, July 29, 2008, you are
all scheduled to take the New York State Bar Exam."

"Do you have any idea who I am?"

THE SEVENTH DECADE
1985-1994

THE *SEVENTH* DECADE
1985-1994

MARK SINGER

*"Listen, I have money on the other line.
Can I call you back?"*

I'm an agnostic when it comes to the data about alleged productivity increases in recent years, because I recall the mid-eighties as a time when it was theoretically possible to get a lot more done. For starters, the average day then lasted about thirty-six hours. (Around my house, empirical proof of this proposition was signified by numbers of small children underfoot and corollary units of sleep deprivation—inspiration for my motto "Thank God it's Monday.") I wasn't the only one who needed a little down time; Ronald Reagan, the great communicator, was rarely more eloquent than when he dozed off during cabinet meetings (and, unless I misremember, occasionally during press conferences). In 1986, Mick Stevens populated a captionless gag with a half-dozen somnolent customers and a snoozing proprietor inside a diner identified as "The Decafé." I wanted to crawl inside that cartoon.

As the eighties blended into the nineties, a glut of bloated, easy targets accumulated: beyond-shameless avarice (Ivan Boesky, Donald Trump, Michael Milken, Imelda and Ferdinand Marcos, Leona Helmsley); awe-inspiring ecclesiastical hypocrisy (the defrocked televangelists Jim Bakker and Jimmy Swaggart); inane adventurism (the Iran-Contra affair); and is-this-a-great-country-or-what everyday gaucherie. But a professional satirist had to cope with some novel, inconvenient workplace conditions, including an inhibiting new taxonomy—"politically correct" versus whatever wasn't—that had been superimposed upon the collective awareness. From a different direction, the bar was raised by the advent of "The Simpsons," Western civilization's singular twentieth-century achievement (with the exception, naturally, of *The New Yorker* cartoon).

Meanwhile, genuine evil was gruesomely on the loose—the perpetrators of the first World Trade Center bombing, the terrorists who brought down Pan Am flight 103, Jeffrey Dahmer, John Gotti, the loner du jour armed with an automatic weapon or two. The AIDS epidemic exploded and the hole in the ozone layer expanded. Cigarette smoking declined but antidepressant consumption shot up, along with sexual-harassment claims. So what was there to laugh about? Plenty of fresh unsettling or outright appalling stuff: cloning, portable phones and fax machines and assorted high-tech gadgetry and jargon, name-brandism amok, the democratization of celebrity, greed, and amorality.

(One of Richard Cline's jaded sophisticates, talking on his portable phone while standing on the deck of a beach house, says, "Listen, I have money on the other line. Can I call you back?") Most of the *New Yorker* cartoons of that era, including the catapults beyond reality of Barsotti, Ziegler, et al., reflected the binary choice between the dreadful and the absurd.

Which is why, among other reasons, psychotherapy remained a cartoon growth industry. Danny Shanahan's 1989 two-panel classic (A: "Lassie! Get help!" B: Lassie supine on the shrink's couch) was a reminder that the patient had made only marginal, if any, progress toward a cure. The legal and medical professions also hung in there as reliable foils ("My son the lawyer is suing my son the doctor for malpractice"—yes!, Edward Frascino), joined by briefcased yuppies. The splendid Steiner, again: a herd of nerds in business suits, as dull and docile as cattle, idle inside a feedlot pen as, on the other side of the fence, one rustic in overalls says to another, "In six more weeks, these M.B.A.s will be ready for market." The invigorating twist was that the nerds weren't exclusively male. For longer than necessary (caveat: in making the following assertion, I'm deliberately ignoring Roz Chast's egalitarian confederacy of neurotics and obsessives), men had cornered the market on zhlubbiness, tactlessness, and general lameness. Not that guys weren't still masters of the craft: a cheerful cad in a Mick Stevens cocktail-party scene tells a perky gal, "Now, you wait right here while I go ask my wife for a divorce." Yet one reassuring measure of social progress was that women were at last free to be fatuous not only as self-esteem-mongering mommies but *on the job*.

I would maintain that Robert Mankoff's 1993 "No, Thursday's out. How about never—is never good for you?" is the quintessential encapsulation of the decade. Feel free to quibble or, if it makes you happier, sue me. Or perhaps we could simply agree to empathize with all the characters in Tom Cheney's 1989 bedroom scene: timid soul with mustache, wearing striped pajamas, stands next to the bed of an elderly couple and is informed, "Son, your mother and I think that you are now old enough to get your own drink of water." Indeed. But how is he going to get back to sleep?

"No, Thursday's out. How about never—is never good for you?"

"One of the boys racked up your car, Mr. McVinney, so in all
fairness we're going to return your Christmas gift."

"Now, you wait right here while I go ask my wife for a divorce."

Nature Girl
and the Four Elements

EARTH

WATER

FIRE

AIR

*"And now at this point in the meeting I'd like to shift
the blame away from me and onto someone else."*

THE DAWN OF TIME

"Please, John, not the cheap Scotch. My body is a temple."

"Thanks for waiting for me, Jocko, but I still can't play.
I've decided to go for a Ph.D."

"Now, brighten up. You know you'll have fun. The men
will fear you, and the women will adore you."

"I don't mind your acting as your own attorney, but would you
please stop hopping on and off that damned chair?"

Animal Magnetism

*"The bidding will start at
eleven million dollars."*

"You mean no one remembered to bring a rock?"

"How about some little pads and pencils?"

"He's my best friend and he works hard all day.
Couldn't you at least wag your tail?"

"Lights! Cameras! Christmas!"

"Finish it? Why would I want to finish it?"

"We hate to shop."

VACATION ENDS
1 MILE

"While you were out, Stevie Wonder just called to say he loves you."

LARGE, GREAT, HUGE, CONSIDERABLE, BULKY, VOLUMINOUS, AMPLE, MASSIVE, CAPACIOUS, SPACIOUS, MIGHTY, TOWERING, MONSTROUS...

ROGET'S BRONTOSAURUS

"I received two anonymous valentines. One, I fancy, was from you."

"That is the correct answer, Billy, but I'm afraid
you don't win anything for it."

"Let's just go in and see what happens."

"There's more inside."

"Look, I'm not saying it's going to be today. But someday—someday—
you guys will be happy that you've taken along a lawyer."

1986

"I'm a social scientist, Michael. That means I can't explain electricity or anything like that, but if you ever want to know about people I'm your man."

"Call it vanity, call it narcissism, call it egomania. I love you."

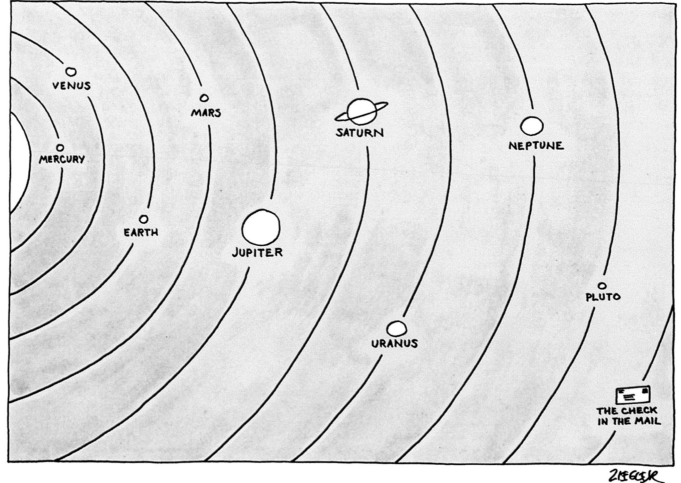

"Got it!"

"I'm walking!"

"Art, you're beautiful, but you have three minutes."

NEW YORK'S NEWEST NEIGHBORHOOD~
Little Vermont

R. Chast

"Why am I talking this loud? Because I'm wrong."

"No, this is not the 12:38 to Bridgeport."

THE DECAFÉ

"Every man for himself!"

THANKSGIVING ← ←   CHRISTMAS NEXT RIGHT   NEW YEAR'S SECOND RIGHT   AHEAD SUPER BOWL SUNDAY

"By God, for a minute there it
suddenly all made sense!"

STORES OF MYSTERY

Fred's Drugs

Surrounded by cut-rate drug-and-cosmetic emporiums that sell, let's say, a bottle of XYZ shampoo for 79¢. Same bottle at Fred's? $2.09!!! How does he do it?

Beauty-Moi Frocks

Weird clothes, always five seasons out of date. Has been there forever. Store is usually pretty empty except for racks and racks of pants suits and the like. Who shops here?

M + O Typewriter Supplies

This place has been closed whenever one has walked by it. However, it's _always_ _there_, meaning somebody is continuing to pay rent on it. Why?

Tip-Top Goods

Boxes of saltines next to cartons of hair spray. Wigs, Christmas decorations, halter tops, institutional-sized jars of olives. Did all of this stuff "fall off a truck" or what?

r. Chast

THE FIRST STRAW

MANKOFF

"Mind if I put on the game?"

"Feel that invisible push? That's New York."

"You moved."

RADIATOR COOKERY

Flounder: 2 days

Potato: 3 weeks, 5 days

12 lb. roast: 4 months, 9 days

"It's wonderful, darling. It really says Manhattan."

Difficult Letter

"We're still pretty far apart. I'm looking for a six-figure advance
and they're refusing to read the manuscript."

"Our real first line of defense, wouldn't you agree, is our capacity to reason."

"I knew you'd like this place."

SAFE SEX

"Let me take you away from all this and bring you over to all that."

"It just seems to me, Howard, that you're missing the whole point of having a terrace in the city."

"Could you walk a little faster, buddy? This is New York."

"Finally, let me put to rest the so-called 'character' issue."

"This year, tax reform has radically changed the federal tables and methods for calculating withholding taxes."

"I thought I'd give Western medicine one more chance."

"Frankly, I think we'll regret introducing these organisms into the environment."

BEFORE   AFTER

"I'll have an ounce of prevention."

"I *told* him to lay off the high-fibre diet."

"I thought I loved it, but Gordon said
we were just manipulated."

"Fredric W. Desbrow & Son, plumbers."

Little Things

chent · spak · kabe · tiv · redge · kellat · enker · bie · sood · hackeb

R. Chast

DONNA KARAN'S NIGHTMARE

DKNJ

R. Chast

THE VELCROS AT HOME

R. Chast

ROZ CHAST

Roz Chast's drawings tiptoed into *The New Yorker* in 1978 with a whisper that quickly grew to a roar. Readers were puzzled, then indignant, then outraged. Letters flooded into the magazine, some suggesting that the artist must be blackmailing the publisher. Even some cartoonists, normally a collegial lot, were upset. What was going on? The answer goes to the heart of Chast's genius. Her work upset readers' expectations; her gently stylized drawings were not really "cartoons" and her ideas were not really "gags." Jack Ziegler refined the conventions of the *New Yorker* cartoon, but Roz Chast threw them out the window.

Gradually, the furor abated. As it turned out, Chast's parallel universe was remarkably like our own, only funnier. Who wouldn't want to purchase get-well-soon cards for their appliances? Or clip recipes for radiator cookery? Or, best of all, find the best viewing spot for the Tournament of Neuroses Parade?

Chast should not be confused with one of the hapless neurotics who populate her meta-world. She is a happily married suburban mother of two, and, although she describes herself as "not Ms. Bubbly," her darkened studio (she willfully keeps the blinds drawn) is far removed from the drab walkups of her drawings. William Shawn, a great admirer of her work, once wondered aloud if she could keep it up. Twenty-five years later, the question is moot. Until the gene for quiet desperation is isolated and excised, Roz Chast will remain the indispensable guide for the perplexed.

BAR BAR

THE DIALOGUES OF PLATO

Phrieda: Plato, what do you want for lunch?

Plato: Anything. Whatever.

Phrieda: How's tuna?

Plato: Not tuna.

Phrieda: I could make you some scrambled eggs.

Plato: Grilled cheese.

Phrieda: We don't have any cheese.

Plato: I want grilled cheese!

Phrieda: I'll go to the store later and buy some cheese, but right now we don't have any cheese, so tell me: what do you want for lunch?

Plato: I don't want anything.

Phrieda: You have to have something.

Plato: You can't force me.

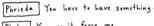

TWO MORE POEMS from TED HUGHES

I once knew a lady from Mass.
Who was sometimes a pain in the ass.
Every damn comma
Was really high drama,
But she was quite a talented lass.

Sylvia Plath was my mate,
She and I went on a date.
She learned how to cook,
Then published a book,
And the rest is all up for debate.

MIDDLE AGE

THE MAGAZINE FOR YOU - YEAH, YOU!

See That Old Lady Sitting Across From You? That's How You Look, Too.

"I Was the Oldest Person at the Dead Concert": A SPECIAL REPORT

So You've Turned Into Your Dad.

THE WORLD'S #1 MOTIVATIONAL SPEAKER

Make me proud before I die.

I'm begging.

1988

"We laugh at the same things."

"Hi, Dad. Investment banking wasn't that great after all."

"We had her declawed, but she's still impossible."

"If I may, Mr. Perlmutter, I'd like to answer your question *with* a question."

"I told him it wouldn't kill him to try to be nice
once in a while, but I was wrong."

*"So far so good.
Let's hope we win."*

"No, no, Senator, no thanks are necessary at this time."

*"It's got to come out, of course, but that doesn't
address the deeper problem."*

"Makes you wonder, doesn't it?"

"You're not one of those guys who are
afraid of intimacy, are you?"

"And *your* problems will always be my problems, Wendy—
except when I'm really, *really* busy."

"Mrs. Hammond! I'd know you anywhere
from little Billy's portrait of you."

"The poor are getting poorer, but with the rich getting
richer it all averages out in the long run."

"Mr. Hoffman? Ed Hoffman? Your office has been trying to reach you, sir."

MOSES IN CONNECTICUT

"This CD player costs less than players selling for twice as much."

"I still don't have all the answers, but I'm beginning
to ask the right questions."

"We'll begin, Mr. Bergeron, just as soon as you're seated."

KONG FOR A DAY

NATURE'S GREATEST CONFLICTS

KILLER WHALE
vs.
KILLER BEE

You better watch your step, pal.

Aaaangh, you think you're such a tough guy.

HIPPOSUCTION

BEFORE

AFTER

"Well, your jersey damn sure wasn't inside out when you left home this morning."

"The chicken is for this year's taxes.
The egg is my estimated for next year."

TO DO
1. Call Bank
2. Dry Cleaner
3. Forge in the smithy of my soul the uncreated conscience of my race.
4. Call mom

JAMES JOYCE'S REFRIGERATOR

"Hey, do you want to be on the news tonight or not?
This is a sound bite, not the Gettysburg Address. Just say what
you have to say, Senator, and get the hell off."

"How very exciting! I have never before
met a _Second_ Amendment lawyer."

"Shouldn't he be lying at the _foot_ of the bed?"

"Frankly, I'm looking for something that might appeal to a jury."

"They have very strict anti-pollution laws in this state."

"Son, your mother and I think that you are now old enough to get your own drink of water."

"My fees are quite high, and yet you say you have little money. I think I'm seeing a conflict of interest here."

"Would everyone check to see they have an attorney? I seem to have ended up with two."

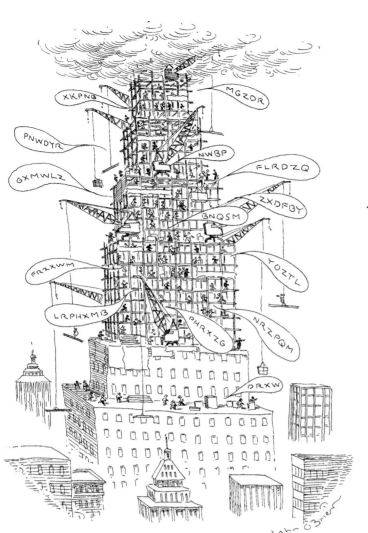

"Well, the children are grown up, married, divorced, and remarried. I guess our job is done."

THE STAT FAMILY

"I didn't realize, Your Honor. I assumed the law here was the same as in New Jersey. As you may know, dog eat dog is permissible there."

Suspense

MARTHA STEWART TAKES OVER THE UNIVERSE

Formal Dinner for Twenty-four on Mars

Make sure your lighting is apropos!

Sunday Brunch for Eight on Pluto

Freshly cut flowers are a must!

Ultra-Perfect Christmas Feast for Two Hundred in Alpha Centauri System

Don't forget the personalized finger bowls!

"It's always 'Sit,' 'Stay,' 'Heel'—never
'Think,' 'Innovate,' 'Be yourself.'"

"I think globally, but I spend locally."

531

"We try to set aside a little time for silliness."

"While you were on vacation, Zooker, a motion was made and seconded to saw five and a half inches off your chair legs."

"Oh-oh, we're in trouble!"

"I'd like to hear less talk about animal rights and more talk about animal responsibilities."

MODERN MEDICINE

"Well, Bob, it looks like a paper cut, but just to be sure let's do lots of tests."

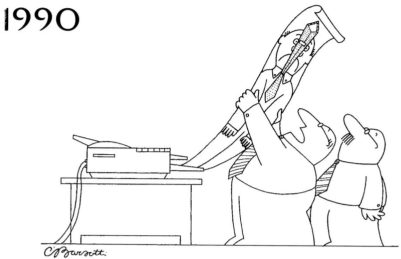

"My God, there's been a terrible accident in our Chicago office!"

"Nice talking to you, Al!"

"We have two offices throughout the world."

MENTAL BAGGAGE CLAIM

Excuse me, I believe I see my resentment of physical beauty.

Those lifelong regrets about stopping ballet lessons when I was ten? Those are mine.

Oh, there's my hypochondria coming out right now.

"The doctor is in court on Tuesdays and Wednesdays."

"To answer your question. Yes, if you shoot an arrow into the air and it falls to earth you know not where, you could be liable for any damage it may cause."

"You came up in therapy today."

"Good morning. I'm Craig Nisbet, and I'm trying to meet women."

"Certainly. A party of four at seven-thirty in the name of Dr. Jennings. May I ask whether that is an actual medical degree or merely a Ph.D.?"

"According to this, everything we've done up to now is right."

"Well, I'm employed by them, but I'm working for me."

"Do you, Scofield Industries, take Amalgamated Pipe?"

"It's so lovely out here you wonder why they have it so far from the city."

"O.K., Mr. Spinelli, you're up. Now bank her to the right, and I'll talk you back in for a nice smooth landing."

"This is going to be kind of a working lunch."

THAT'S IT, PAL. NO MORE WORK FOR YOU.

WORKAHOLICS

"Why do you think you cross the road?"

"My people will get back to your people."

"My son the lawyer is suing my son
the doctor for malpractice."

"Mr. Smith's office doesn't have a door. You have to
batter your way through the wall."

THE SEVEN DWARFS AFTER THERAPY

"Don't worry. Fantasies about devouring
the doctor are perfectly normal."

"I'm having an out-of-money experience."

"Stand aside, Gruenwald! It's the computer I'm blowing away!"

"Not only do you look marvellous but all of you looks the same age."

"Of course you're going to be depressed if you keep comparing yourself with successful people."

"When was the last time you started her up?"

"We got a great buy on the apartment, but, unfortunately, it didn't include the mineral rights."

THE FOUR AGES OF MAN

INFANCY   CHILDHOOD   YOUTH   MATURITY

"Curiosity."

"My question is: Are we making an impact?"

"Don't say a word! Your eyes, your hair, your T-shirt,
your luggage—they say it all."

"So, while extortion, racketeering, and murder may be
bad acts, they don't make you a bad person."

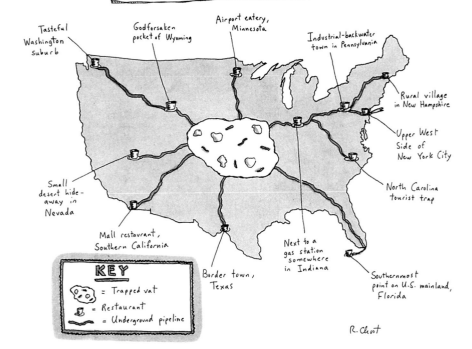

THE HUGE-UNDERGROUND-TRAPPED-VAT
THEORY OF WHY ALL WONTON SOUP TASTES
EXACTLY THE SAME

Tasteful
Washington
suburb

Godforsaken
pocket of Wyoming

Airport eatery,
Minnesota

Industrial-backwater
town in Pennsylvania

Rural village
in New Hampshire

Upper West
Side of
New York City

North Carolina
tourist trap

Small
desert hide-
away in
Nevada

Mall restaurant,
Southern California

Border town,
Texas

Next to a
gas station
somewhere
in Indiana

Southernmost
point on U.S. mainland,
Florida

KEY

= Trapped vat

= Restaurant

= Underground pipeline

R. Chast

"Honest, Martha, I don't mean to crowd you."

"You smell like a chimney."

*"During the next stage of my development, Dad, I'll be drawing
closer to my mother—I'll get back to you in my teens."*

Business cartoons became a staple of *The New Yorker* in the thirties, and the magazines of the fifties were filled with them: boardrooms, back rooms, organization men, men in gray flannel suits. But, as the business world began to change, the cartoons had to shift as well. Many of the old comic portraits of business became obsolete. Cartoons from earlier in the century that showed men greeted at the front door, at the end of a hard day at the office, by their stay-at-home wives, for example, lost legitimacy when women began to enter the workplace. And in the eighties business cartoons often turned on the conflation of the office space and the home space. Portable technologies, from cell phones to laptops, made it easy to bring work home, and the materialist culture of the Reagan era made work more important than it had been in years. Personal relationships and neuroses, more than ever, found their way into offices. Business invaded the home. Perhaps the pithiest (and most pessimistic) articulation of the ubiquity of business culture came in 1993, when Richard Cline drew a cartoon of two businessmen talking. "And before you know it," one says, "you're looking at everyone as a commission."

"Couldn't you, just once, leave that face at the office?"

SUITABLE FOR HOME OR OFFICE USE

"And after the prime rate declined by half a point, and the Dow rose by thirty-two, guess what happened to Goose and Fox?"

"Edmund works at home."

"And before you know it you're looking at everyone as a commission."

"Actually, Lou, I think it was more than just my being in the right place at the right time. I think it was my being the right race, the right religion, the right sex, the right socioeconomic group, having the right accent, the right clothes, going to the right schools . . ."

"That's it. I'm taking the buyout."

"Has it ever occurred to you just to say, 'Hey, I quit. I don't want to be a part of the food chain anymore'?"

"All you really need in life is the love of a good cat."

"Wentworth, could I take another look at that reorganization plan?"

GODZILLA MEETS MOZZARELLA

WHERE EARL GETS HIS IDEAS

547

"*If you lie down with pugs, you wake up with pugs.*"

"*Gotta run, sweetheart. By the way, that was one fabulous job you did raising the children.*"

"Résumés over there."

"Pendleton, as of noon today your services will no longer be required. Meanwhile, keep up the good work."

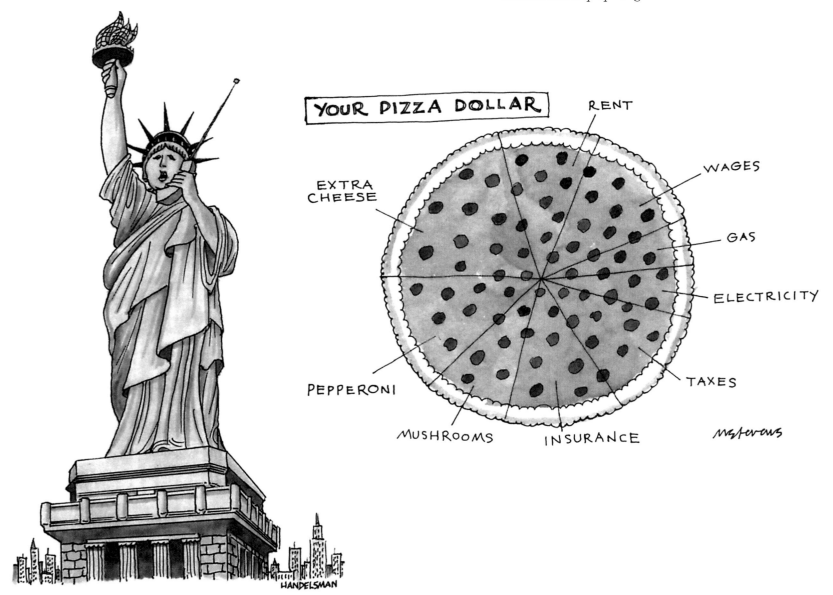

"Well, it all depends. Where are these huddled masses coming from?"

YOUR PIZZA DOLLAR

RENT

WAGES

GAS

ELECTRICITY

TAXES

INSURANCE

MUSHROOMS

PEPPERONI

EXTRA CHEESE

"I couldn't sleep."

"I've got the bowl, the bone, the big yard.
I know I should be happy."

"The ringing in your ears—I think I can help."

"But how do you know for sure you've got power unless you abuse it?"

IN DEEP DENIAL

"I'm not asking you to change your spots. I'm just asking you to take out the garbage."

"In six more weeks, these M.B.A.s will be ready for market."

"Of course, with the position that has the benefits— medical, dental, et cetera—there is no salary."

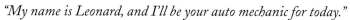

"My name is Leonard, and I'll be your auto mechanic for today."

"English lit—how about you?"

552

"The point is to get so much money that money's not the point anymore."

"Is there any chance of getting my testicles back?"

"We are neither hunters nor gatherers. We are accountants."

"Why, you're right. Tonight isn't reading night, tonight is sex night."

"I have a brief statement, a clarification, and two denials."

"No, not there, please. That's where I'm going to put my head."

1993

"We're shopping around for a new agency, and we thought you people might be interested in making a pitch."

"I may have something rather outside your field.
Would you consider indentured servitude?"

"According to an article in the upcoming issue of 'The New England
Journal of Medicine,' all your fears are well founded."

"Oh, not bad. The light comes on, I press the bar,
they write me a check. How about you?"

"For heaven's sake, Melissa, she's my mother. I can't tell her to leave."

"*What I don't get is why once we fly south we don't just <u>stay</u> there.*"

" '*How I Spent My Summer Vacation,*' *by Lilia Anya, all rights reserved, which includes the right to reproduce this essay or portions thereof in any form whatsoever, including, but not limited to, novel, screenplay, musical, television miniseries, home video, and interactive CD-*ROM."

"*We're borrowing the best features of the Canadian system.*"

"What's amazing to me is that this late in the game we _still_ have to settle our differences with rocks."

"It's not you, Rob. It's just that things are moving a little too fast."

"Well, Stoddard, I think I've bounced enough ideas off you for one day."

"Well, I do have this recurring dream that one day I might see some results."

"I'll quit when it stops being fun."

"We used to entertain a great deal."

"Excuse me, I'm lost. Can you direct me to the information superhighway?"

"Whenever Mother's Day rolls around, I regret having eaten my young."

"They're baby boomers—like, you know, really old."

T.S. ELIOT MEETS BEAVIS AND BUTT-HEAD

April sucks.

"You're right. It does send a powerful message."

"You abducted him—you feed him."

"No caffè latte? And you call yourselves a bookstore?"

"Fenwick, Benton & Perkins. How may I direct your call?"

"I'm sorry, we've had to drop the traditional last cigarette, on account of complaints from the firing squad about secondhand smoke."

"Oh, yes, indeed. We all keep a sharp eye out for those little clues that seem to whisper 'law' or 'medicine.'"

HUMAN-RIGHTS ISSUES ASIDE, YOU WILL SOON ENJOY THE BENEFITS OF TRADE WITH CHINA.

"Your oil's fine, but your blood-sugar level's a little low."

"I'm talking so much about books I haven't read
I feel like I'm back in publishing."

"It was so depressing. When I go to the theatre,
I want to be entertained."

"Fusilli, you crazy bastard! How are you?"

NEW FROM THE MAKERS OF THE WONDERBRA.

THE WONDERWALLET.

I know there's only seven bucks in here — but it looks like seven hundred!

"Now you're probably all asking yourselves, 'Why must I learn to read and write?'"

"Well, you don't look like an experimental psychologist to me."

S. GROSS

"The figures for the last quarter are in. We made significant gains in the fifteen-to-twenty-six-year-old age group, but we lost our immortal souls."

"I'm down to two hundred and sixty-three packs a day."

"The free-range chicken with little shoes by Reebok."

"No comment."

THE EIGHTH DECADE
1995-2006

THE EIGHTH DECADE
1995-2006
REBECCA MEAD

"I don't know about you guys, but I don't feel like I've lost one goddam bit of my femininity."

"How long has the Oval Office had a mirror on the ceiling?"

The nineteen-nineties have been characterized as the world's most prosperous decade by the Nobel Prize winner Joseph Stiglitz, who, having been the World Bank's chief economist for part of them, should be in a position to know. That the nineties were also the world's most preposterous decade is a less easily quantifiable proposition, but a case can certainly be made. There was, for example, the transparent silliness of Wall Street during the dot-com boom, when old-fashioned business-model concepts such as the desirability of a revenue stream were lightheartedly cast off like a winter coat on the first day of spring. In domestic political life, too, a hitherto undreamed-of realm of absurdity was entered upon with the President's office romance and the enforced acquaintance, on the part of the American public, with a stained blue dress, Linda Tripp, and all those lies. (Meanwhile, voting machines in Broward County were silently marshalling themselves for vast systemic failure.) Most topsy-turvy of all was the way in which the government, by avidly preparing for the brightly named Millennium Bug while bungling intelligence reports from murkier sources, readied the nation for entirely the wrong disaster.

This was an era when it had never been so necessary to sustain simultaneously a sense of conviction and a sense of implausibility, and *The New Yorker's* cartoonists were busy doing what *The New Yorker's* cartoonists usually do best: commenting on the small-scale comedy of manners of everyday life. Thus, when it came to the sexual-political debacle of Clinton's final days in office, the cartoons were predictive rather than reactive: the precise ludic possibilities presented by Monica Lewinsky were left to the political dailies, while artists like William Hamilton (who in 1996 drew a woman saying to two friends, "I don't know about you guys, but I don't feel like I've lost one goddam bit of my femininity") had been busy showing how Lewinsky got the balls to thong the President in the first place. The first baby boomers' astonished boo-hooing about reaching the qualifying age for membership of A.A.R.P.; the hypocrisies of a business culture that enriched the richest and insulted everyone else; the intractable contradictions of courtship, and the inevitable weariness of enduring marriage: all these were the cartoonists' subject.

In the nineties, and the zero years that followed, Viagra and

Botox made their appearance on druggists' shelves and in *New Yorker* cartoons. (One Roz Chast drawing included Viagra, Prozac, Claritin, Ritalin, Zantac, Xanax, and a half-dozen other pharmacological signs of the times.) The madness of the money culture—surely everyone knew all along that a day trader had about as much claim to credibility as a day surgeon or a day astronaut?—provided rich material; and so did the small meannesses of corporate life disguised as large blandishments, such as the rise of the H.M.O. (Psychoanalysis continues as a *New Yorker* cartoon conceit even after managed care has helped to reduce its widespread practice to a quaint remembrance.) One of the defining characteristics of the age was a pronounced child-centricity, and, if the cartoons of the nineteen-thirties, with their highballs and hangovers, showed how New Yorkers fooled around after the children had been packed off to bed, the cartoonists of the nineteen-nineties captured modern parenthood in all its self-congratulatory drudgery.

The issue of *The New Yorker* that appeared on September 17, 2001, was the first to omit cartoons from its feature pages since 1946, when John Hersey's "Hiroshima" appeared. The cartoons are, along with The Talk of the Town, the most New Yorkish part of *The New Yorker*, and, while the national cataclysm of, say, Presidential perjury, may not have been the cartoonists' particular province, this more immediate trauma was. In the months subsequent to the destruction of the World Trade Center, the cartoons were where you could look for what it was O.K. to say. (By November, 2001, according to the sublime Bruce Eric Kaplan, "It's hard, but slowly I'm getting back to hating everyone.") President Bush's wars in Afghanistan and Iraq have been left largely to *The New Yorker's* writers; but his war against the less conveniently smart-bomb-able territory of "terror" is ideally suited to the art of the cartoonist. "We're from the F.B.I., going from house to house making sure that everyone is scared shitless," say two smiling agents in a cartoon by J. B. Handelsman from November, 2001. The current decade is only half concluded; unimagined preposterousness may be still to come.

"I figure if I don't have that third Martini, then the terrorists win."

"You'll like my parents. They're very child-centered."

"Look, you've got to accept some curtailment of your freedom in exchange for increased security."

"Will you call me?"

"Harmon was shaving and his stomach fell into the sink."

"No giblets, but there's an organ-donor card."

"Human Resources."

"You don't get it, Daddy, because they're not targeting you."

THE LOVE SONG OF

J. ALFRED CREW

I grow old... I grow old... I shall wear the bottoms of my relaxed-fit, button-fly, size-38, in Wheat, trousers rolled.

I shall wear white flannel trousers, back-ordered until May 19th, and walk upon the beach.

"It's a cat calendar, so it may not be all that accurate."

"He's, like, 'To be or not to be,' and I'm, like, 'Get a life.'"

"You may well be from Mars, but the children
and I are still from Westchester."

"Woulda, coulda, shoulda. Next!"

"It's always poor you, isn't it, Albert?"

"As a matter of fact, you did catch us at a bad time."

"Your father and I want to explain why we've decided to live apart."

"Travel is the sherbet between courses of reality."

575

"*They moved my bowl.*"

"*It's a guy thing.*"

"*I have a couple of other
projects I'm excited about.*"

"Are we thinking here, or is this just so much pointing and clicking?"

"You've been around here longer than I have. What <u>are</u> 'congressional ethics'?"

"Oh, the usual. Lunch at Le Cirque and then the abyss."

"We just haven't been flapping them hard enough."

"In the interest of streamlining the judicial process, we'll skip the evidence and go directly to sentencing."

"You are entitled to one call, one fax, or one E-mail."

"What the hell was I supposed to do? I've been declawed!"

"Hate to bother you, but are you getting our supertitles for 'Rigoletto'?"

"Your mother and I think it's time you got a place of your own.
We'd like a little time alone before we die."

EXECUTIVE SOFTBALL LEAGUE

SOMEBODY PICK THAT UP!

"There's someone I'd like you to meet."

"Happy fortieth. I'll take the muscle tone in your upper arms, the girlish timbre of your voice, your amazing tolerance for caffeine, and your ability to digest French fries. The rest of you can stay."

"No, the computers are up. We're down."

"I just figured it out—
we're in the cheap seats."

"Why does _he_ always get to be the boy?"

"As soon as one problem is solved,
another rears its ugly head."

"Do me a favor before you come to bed, Ted. Get dressed."

Dear diary,
Sorry to
bother you again.

LOW SELF-ESTEEM

"I'll have someone from my generation get in touch
with someone from your generation."

"They're a perfect match—she's high-maintenance, and he can fix anything."

"This is Mrs. McBride from marketing."

"After the judicial system, I'm my own harshest critic."

"Some kids at school called you a feminist, Mom, but I punched them out."

"O.K., the third of July is out. How about the fourth?"

583

1996

"As I get older, I find I rely more and more on these sticky notes to remind me."

"How's the squid?"

COLLECT THE ENTIRE SET!

"How will you ever know whether you're a flying
squirrel if you don't give it a shot?"

"Could you write, 'To Penny, my darling ex-wife,
who nurtured me and supported me all through my struggles
as a fledgling writer, and whom I blew off the
minute I had my first big success.'"

"Let's stop this before we both say a lot of things we mean."

"Do you remember, Peg—are we on our way out or on our way back?"

"I'd invite you in, but my life's a mess."

"You promise I won't be the only trophy wife at this thing?"

"I think that just my being here is a big mistake."

"Recess is over, Your Honor."

"Paper or plastic?"

1997

"Scotch and toilet water?"

"It's so much easier now that the children are our age."

"I usually wake up screaming at six-thirty,
and I'm in my office by nine."

"It started out with lactose, but now he's intolerant of _everything_."

"Is this a good time to bring up a car problem?"

"So, are you still with the same parents?"

WHAT LEMMINGS BELIEVE

"Discouraging data on the antidepressant."

"Do you have a minute to talk about your retirement years?"

"Hey, pal, do you have any idea who I think I am?"

"That's it, Henry—you've dialled your last mattress!"

"Goodnight moon. Goodnight house. Goodnight breasts."

JIMMY, SIXTH-GENERATION PAIN IN THE ASS

"I went by the pet store this morning, just for a peek."

*"Which one would you like—'My Life,' the director's cut,
or 'My Life,' for general release?"*

"I may be awhile. I'm soliciting funds for my reëlection campaign."

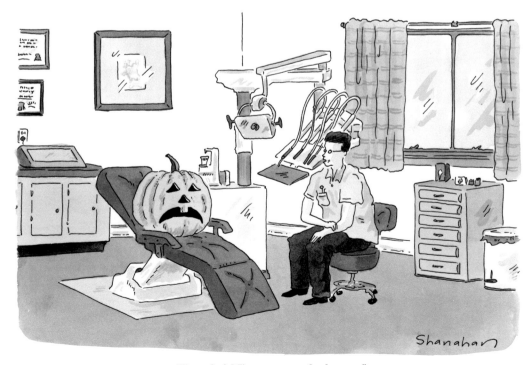

"I'm afraid I've got some bad news."

BRUCE ERIC KAPLAN

SURPRISE PARTY

"It's hard, but slowly I'm getting back to hating everyone."

"In my day, people died."

The New Yorker's cartoons have often been dark, but the drawings of Bruce Eric Kaplan ("BEK") make the Addams Family look like the Brady Bunch. Kaplan's people bicker and kvetch in a spare, Beckett-like universe whose ontological principle seems to be "Life sucks." The popularity of his work suggests that this view is more widely held among our readers than one might imagine, or, rather, hope.

Kaplan has crafted a style that fits this dystopian vision like a death mask—what might be called metro retro. The action, such as it is, is confined within carefully outlined rectangles, lit by the kind of blinding light that precedes alien encounters in science-fiction shows. The furniture is solid but slightly askew, as are the people: like Little Orphan Annie, they lack eyeballs, and their shapeless hands sprout digits only when finger-pointing is called for. Kaplan's signature couple, a pair of cranks, are, aside from their clothes and hairdos, identical: he has slipped same-sex marriage into *The New Yorker*.

Kaplan sold his first drawing to the magazine in 1991. Today, with "cartoon marketplace" an oxymoron, he is one of those lucky artists who don't support themselves solely at the drawing board. He is a successful writer for television, with credits that include several episodes of "Seinfeld," and is an executive producer of "Six Feet Under."

How Kaplan's work will look fifty years on is anyone's guess. Over the years, *New Yorker* artists have produced many memorable creations, and some of the best—Arno's chorus girls, Hokinson's clubwomen, Price's curmudgeons—might have seemed to have limited shelf lives but have endured. For the moment, however, Kaplan is the most convincing and funniest portraitist we have of a postmodernist psyche still stumbling out from the shambles of the fading twentieth century.

"And this is our child, but we never use him."

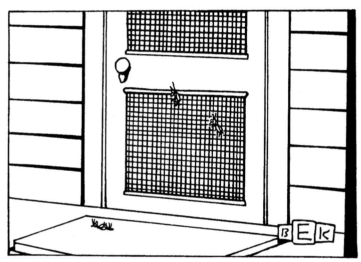

"He will be greatly missed, both on and off the screen."

"I liked it, except for you."

"I'm trying to position myself as loyal."

"If they knew what really went on in hives,
they'd never eat honey again."

"*The men are excited about getting to shoot a lawyer.*"

"Wait, those weren't lies. That was spin!"

"Night fell over the land like an L. L. Bean navy-blue summerweight one-hundred-per-cent-goose-down-filled comforter covering up an Eddie Bauer hunter-green one-hundred-per-cent-combed-cotton, machine-washable king-size fitted sheet."

"Oh, I'm really sorry. I just placed three million with some broker who called five minutes ago."

"Would you like a little phone sex while you hold?"

1998

S. GROSS

"For God's sake, think! Why is he being so nice to you?"

"Never, ever, think outside the box."

INTRODUCING...

THE PILL-OF-THE-MONTH CLUB!

JANUARY	FEBRUARY	MARCH	APRIL
PROZAC	VIAGRA	CLARITIN	EXTRA-STRENGTH TYLENOL
Winter Doldrums	Valentine Vigor!	Hay Fever	Tax Time

MAY	JUNE	JULY	AUGUST
ROGAINE	DEXATRIM	EXCEDRIN	XANAX
The Rites of Spring	Bathing-Suit Season	Kids Home a Lot	Flying Somewhere?

SEPTEMBER	OCTOBER	NOVEMBER	DECEMBER
RITALIN	ESTROGEN	ZANTAC	VALIUM
Back to School!	Autumn Blues	Turkers, etc.	Holiday Overload

R. Chast

"Hey, big guy. Can I buy you a pair of underpants?"

"Scientists confirmed today that everything we know about the
structure of the universe is wrongedy-wrong-wrong."

"I'm so hungry I could eat half a sandwich."

"O.K., I'm sitting. What is it?"

"They're all sons of bitches."

"Can I call you back? I'm shopping."

"And, in this corner, weighing five pounds more than she'd like . . ."

"You don't get an office. You get cargo pants."

"First, they do an on-line search."

S.GROSS

"I don't care if she is a tape dispenser. I love her."

"I have the whole universe to look after, so I'm putting you in charge of this planet."

"No, lad, we aren't movers. We're just Shakers."

"You've got mail."

"Thanks for almost everything, Dad."

"He's dead. Would you like his voice mail?"

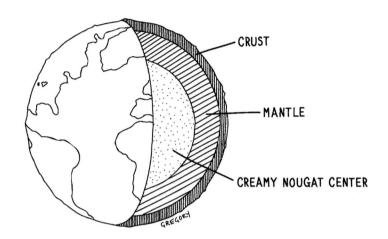

CRUST

MANTLE

CREAMY NOUGAT CENTER

"I don't buy stocks simply because others are buying them.
I buy them because many, many others are buying them."

TODAY:
PARENT/TEACHER
CONFERENCES

"Your daughter is a pain in the ass."

"Stop complaining. Who isn't broke?"

"We're planning on sending him away to be reared by experts."

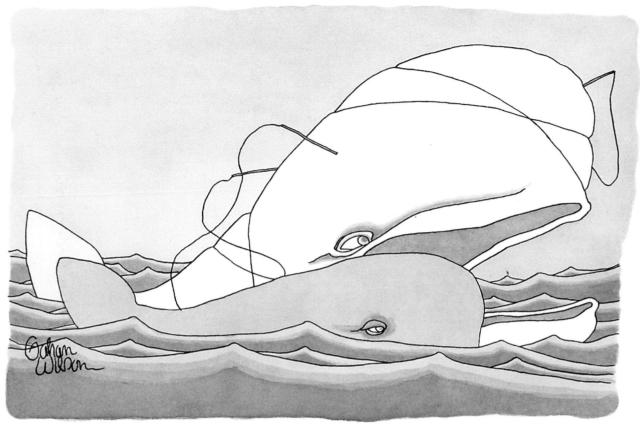

"Now that I've wiped him out, I kind of miss the little peg-legged bastard."

"Luckily, none of the people inside appear to be celebrities."

"The dog ate my magnetic insoles."

SIPRESS

"From right to left, you have your tekkamaki, your futomaki, and then your yamaimo roll. The little pile of pink stuff is ginger, the green one's wasabi. And, of course, you already recognize your vodka Martini."

"Senator, the American people, whom you often mention in your speeches, would like a word with you."

"I know these are things you don't want to hear,
but I'm enjoying the hell out of saying them."

"World War III? Hmm. O.K., but, remember, nobody gets hurt."

"Wunderkinder come and go, but old farts are forever."

"What ever happened to 'Never go to bed angry'?"

2000

"It's an amazing coincidence, isn't it, that we all
served on the same board of directors?"

"Great coffee, honey!"

Sumo on Ice

"This is so cool! I'm flying this thing completely on my Palm pilot!"

"Well, J.B., we're not a successful Internet company because we're not an Internet company."

"There's an article in here that explains why you're such an idiot."

"Your mother wanted you to have this for good luck. It's her foot."

"I guess cats just can't appreciate Frank Gehry."

"So what if he's not the man of your dreams. The 'Times' is going to be there."

"It must be his beeper."

"Gotta be an implant."

"Bond. James Bond."   *"Hell. Go to hell."*

"He's long gone, sheriff—you'll never catch him."

REMEMBER, PHIL: CATCH AND RELEASE.

ANIMALS FOR THE ETHICAL TREATMENT OF PEOPLE

"Welcome to 'All About the Media,'
where members of the media discuss the role of
the media in media coverage of the media."

"Good news, honey—seventy is the new fifty."

"Rufus, here, is the center of our life!"

STOCKOPOLIS

2000

"I understand the Everest climb used to be quite a chore."

"Am I the smart one and you're the pretty
one or is it the other way around?"

"To *you* it was fast."

"I'm sorry, dear. I wasn't listening. Could you repeat
what you've said since we've been married?"

SIPRESS

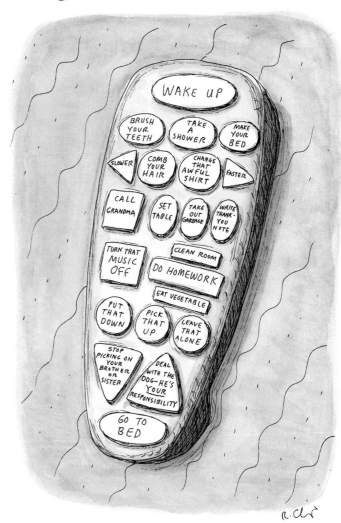

"On the Internet, nobody knows you're a dog."

THE GUY WHO TOOK A WRONG TURN OFF THE ELECTRONIC SUPERHIGHWAY AND WOUND UP IN A MICROWAVE OVEN IN DAVENPORT, IOWA

The first *New Yorker* cartoon about the Internet is also the most famous: Peter Steiner's 1993 panel, which carries the unforgettable caption "On the Internet, nobody knows you're a dog." At the time, the information superhighway (as it was commonly known) was just starting to gain popularity: there was Gopher but no Google, newsgroups but no graphical Web browsers. The technology was almost entirely alien to the American public; in fact, Steiner himself has admitted that he didn't quite know what the caption meant. Still, he somehow perfectly predicted both the Internet's promise and its problems. In those early years, most cartoonists had a straightforward approach: they lampooned the promise of a high-tech panacea. In 1993, Roz Chast pointed out the Internet's similarity to ordinary household appliances, and Donald Reilly lamented its failure to measure up to an old-fashioned lunch. Soon, however, cartoonists were ranging farther afield, and by the late nineties there were jokes about e-mail privacy, dot-coms, online porn, and even search engines. The cartoons include Chast's sketch of some of the characters referred to in spam, Alex Gregory's take on the music-downloading controversy, and Charles Barsotti's snapshot of the twenty-first-century Zeitgeist ("I can't explain it—it's just a funny feeling that I'm being Googled"). One of the best-known *New Yorker* Internet cartoons never appeared in the magazine; rather, it was described in a memorable "Seinfeld" episode in which Elaine visits the magazine's cartoon editor and interrogates him about the meaning of a panel in which a cat says to a dog, "I've enjoyed reading your e-mail"—although that particular episode of the sitcom was written by the *New Yorker* cartoonist Bruce Eric Kaplan.

"I can't explain it—it's just a funny feeling that I'm being Googled."

"I got my ticket for three dollars over the Internet.
Are you going to eat that salmon?"

"Trust me, Mort—no electronic-communications superhighway, no matter
how vast and sophisticated, will ever replace the art of the schmooze."

"I swear I wasn't looking at smut—
I was just stealing music."

"What I don't, like, get is how she, like, figured out I was, like, having an affair with, like, the babysitter."

"Your Honor, if it please the court I'd like to deliver my opening comments in the form of a power ballad."

"You have the wrong number. No one whose name is pronounced that way lives here."

"The suggestions are supposed to go in the box."

"Forty-one years of marriage. That's a long, long, long learning curve."

"You have creepy peasants."

"Good luck with your lecture, Eric—they're loaded for white male."

2001

"You can't handle the meaning of life!"

FRENCH ARMY KNIFE

MR. WRIGHT

"Do you have this in a cat?"

"You're right—things *are* funnier in threes."

"From the violent nature of the multiple stab wounds,
I'd say the victim was probably a consultant."

623

2001

1991 1995 1998 1999 2001

"Honey, your head's through the armhole again."

"It appears to be some kind of wireless technology."

"Honey, let's lay off the Botox for a while, shall we?"

"Sex brought us together, but gender drove us apart."

"Can you recommend a large-breasted
Burgundy with a big behind?"

"We'll need to declaw the cat."

"*Lucy, move—you're blocking Pliny the Elder.*"

"Him? Oh, he's the guy who owns the car."

"You know, in some cultures the male does things."

"We're not doing anything for Gay Pride this year.
We're here, we're queer, we're used to it."

"The sun rises on the Upper East Side and sets on the Upper West Side."

2002

"I think that if these Islamic fundamentalists got to know us they'd like us."

"Once again, man beats machine!"

*"Cathy, this will be an easy sleepover for you—
Ben doesn't take any medications at all."*

"You slept with her, didn't you?"

"I like you, Henry—you're one of the few people around here who actually get it."

"I can't believe it—a punk like me laying off an industry legend like you."

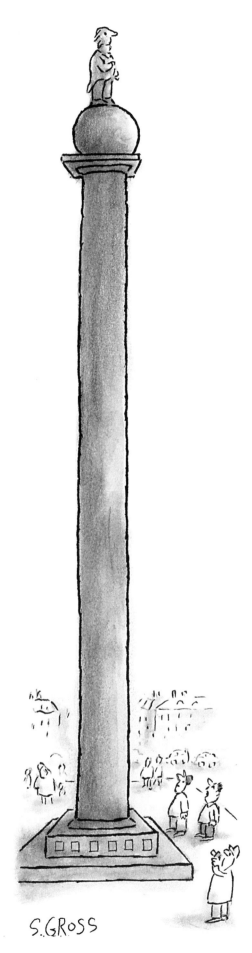

"In real life, he had acrophobia."

629

FOLLOW-UP

"Are we in this Starbucks or the one down the street?"

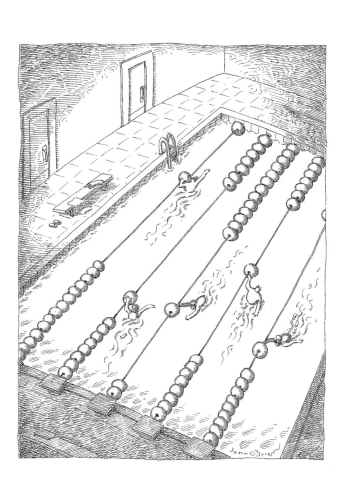

"What I do as an artist is take an ordinary object—say, a lamppost—and, by urinating on it, transform it into something that is uniquely my own."

GREGORY

"On your left."

B. Smaller

"Can we be seated under a vegan painting?"

"What's to prevent some total stranger anywhere
in the world from paying my bills?"

"I'll have the misspelled 'Ceasar' salad and the improperly hyphenated veal osso-buco."

"Wouldn't it be faster if we just flew to Brooklyn?"

"This is sloth—greed is on the top floor."

"I should have bought more crap."

"Yes, I do make things, son. I make things called deals."

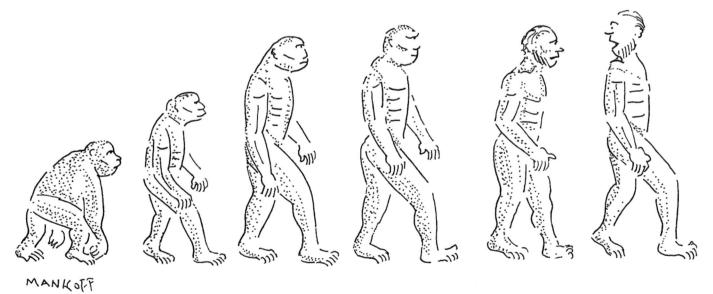

"Hey! Cut out the grab-ass."

"To be on the safe side, let's just say 'noonish.'"

"Braithwaite & Starbucks. How may we help you?"

"Honey, I'm home."

"Before you sentence me, I'd like to remind the court that I was just passing through the building looking for a bathroom."

"T.G.I.F.!"

"If we take a late retirement and an early death, we'll just squeak by."

"Loved the movie. Hated the audience."

"They got extinct because they didn't listen to their mommies."

"Not tonight, hon, I have a concussion."

"I have a taste for luxury."

637

"Sheer will, I tell you—sheer will."

"Walk, hell—I gotta dance!"

"I started my vegetarianism for health reasons, then it became a moral choice, and now it's just to annoy people."

"Sorry, Pop, but your message is no longer relevant to the younger audience."

"Don't come home till that bag is full of money."

"When I think of the as yet undreamed-of loopholes
that are going to be available to you guys!"

"This is what happens when ethical standards
are set artificially high."

"Autumn already? O.K., I'll come down."

"This stuff worked pretty well on me."

"Geez Louise—I left the price tag on."

"I don't have to be a team player, Crawford.
I'm the team owner."

TWO BARBARIANS AND A PROFESSOR OF BARBARIAN STUDIES

"This next blues is about the 5:37 to Scarsdale,
and how it's frequently late, and crowded."

"I need someone well versed in the art of torture—
do you know PowerPoint?"

2003

"We've come here to smoke."

YOUR LOST WEIGHT

"Yes, they are crazy, but they can open the fridge."

"Ready to head back?"

"I'd like your honest, unbiased, and possibly career-ending opinion on something."

*"We're not here to talk about what I want for Christmas—
we're here to talk about what you want for Christmas."*

FINE — IF THEY ALL WANT TO MEET ONLINE, SCREW THEM.

*"Susan, this might be just the wine talking,
but I think I want to order more wine."*

2004

"No, I didn't. I never said there should be _no_ government regulation."

"Many women are more at ease with a female doctor.
That's why I'm wearing the wig."

"Who gets Meals on Wheels?"

"Jimmy Choo, Manolo Blahnik—honestly can't taste the difference."

"Your appointment with the doctor is at eleven-fifteen,
but his appointment with you is at twelve-fifteen."

"Daddy doesn't know any magic tricks. Daddy knows accounting tricks."

2004

The Night Before the Big Meeting Frank Receives a
Visit from the PowerPoint Fairy.

"What wine goes best with vodka?"

"All my lunch money's in real estate."

ZEROTASKING

"So this is where the magic happens."

"It may be wrong, but it's how I feel."

2004

"I'll begin today's proceedings by saying that we have enough food and water to last us until some sort of eventual turnaround."

"We want you to have fun, as long as it's fun that enhances a college-admission application."

"Velcro!"

"It's supposed to ward off frivolous lawsuits."

NAPQUEST

START: YOUR DESK
FINISH: LIVING-ROOM SOFA
EST. DISTANCE: .00008 MILE
EST. TIME: 7.5 SECONDS

① At the end of your chair, make a right.	.00001 mile
② Continue till end of desk and make a sharp left.	.00001 mile
③ Go straight on carpet.	.00003 mile
④ Bear left at end of carpet.	.00002 mile
⑤ Turn left onto sofa.	.00001 mile

"You may now begin your insane experiment."

"*We design them here, but the labor is cheaper in Hell.*"

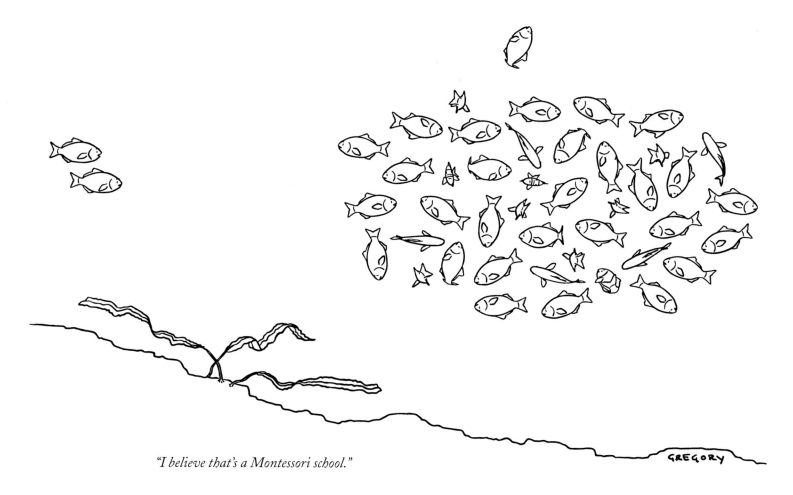

"*I believe that's a Montessori school.*"

"You can say anything you want, or you can say
nothing, but most people say 'Wheeeeee!!!'"

"If I ever say anything I haven't said already, let me know."

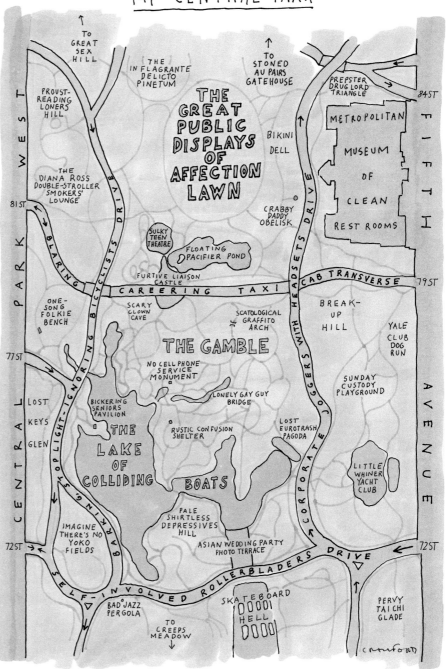

MY CENTRAL PARK

651

2004

"Can you hang on a sec? I think I just took another picture of my ear."

"Hey, this is brilliant! Where do you get my ideas?"

"This next one is a hard-rockin', kick-ass, take-no-prisoners tune we wrote about turning sixty."

"I'll check and see if he's available."

"Gays and lesbians getting married—haven't they suffered enough?"

"Today I'm announcing I've decided to get out of my family so I can devote more time to politics."

"I used to be an idealist, but now I'm an independent."

The artists of *The New Yorker* have long had a reputation for avoiding politics, but the truth is that their cartoons have always been political without being political cartoons. In the magazine's history, there are precious few cartoons that show bears taking swipes at eagles or donkeys at elephants, but there are hundreds that puncture the solemnity of the political system by lampooning puffed-up senators and congressmen—their doubletalk and their false promises. In fact, the political press conference has become a *New Yorker* cartoon standard. In the past decade, though, as national politics has become more personal, the cartoons have looked more closely at the intersection of the two worlds. The Monica Lewinsky scandal, of course, was the source of many jokes: in 1998, Danny Shanahan drew a couple arriving late at a party with an unusual excuse, and Peter Steiner's dominatrix turned down an offer to re-create Monicagate. Soon enough, though, cartoonists, like most Americans, grew weary of the impeachment flap, and they returned to the more oblique brand of politics that had characterized the magazine's humor for decades: names were rarely named, but the issues of the day were raised. One topic that seemed tailor-made for punch lines was the futile search for weapons of mass destruction. The people in cartoons—Alex Gregory's bemused athletes, for instance—felt like the people out of cartoons, alternately defensive about their government and suspicious of it.

"I approve of the way he's mishandling the economy."

"After the whole W.M.D. thing, I don't know *what* to believe."

"Sorry we're late, but Kenneth Starr subpoenaed our regular babysitter."

"I totally agree with you about capitalism, neo-colonialism, and globalization, but you really come down too hard on shopping."

"Are you decent?"

"Remember, we can only afford to do all this pro bono because of how much anti bono pays."

"And this is our department of experimental accounting."

"Can I have a pony?"

"You'll be awake during the entire procedure. The anesthesiologist is on vacation."

"How's everything?"

"He built his own airplane from a kit."

"Do you mind if I give you a little destructive criticism?"

"Understand, Richardson, I don't believe in evolution,
but I do believe in Darwinism."

"Is there a dramaturge in the house?"

"The F.D.A. is nuts about it."

"I'm big in Japan."

"I've spent so much time with family that I've started to lose sight of what really matters."

PETE TOWNSHEND VINEYARDS

"Fetch and roll over weren't enough—then they sent me to philosophy classes."

THE SPECIALS

"Iced grande soy triple-lutz latte!"

"Beauty is life's E-Z Pass."

"Definitely work-related."

"I just want to go home, crawl into bed, and do some more work."

IN VINO
FERTILIZATION

"My first-choice college should have lots of closet space."

*"We've been victorious in many battles, and yet
helmet hair remains our fiercest foe."*

"They're harmless when they're alone, but get a bunch of them together with a research grant and watch out."

"I had my own blog for a while, but I decided to go back to just pointless, incessant barking."

"And remember, if you need anything I'm available 24/6."

"I'll have the chicken Tamiflu."

"Why on earth would you spring for color film?"

"*Call my attorney and say that I killed Ted in self-defense. Call my publicist and say that I wish Ted the best of luck in all his future endeavors.*"

"You know, you can do this just as easily online."

"Uh–oh, your coverage doesn't seem to include illness."

"Were we gay?"

"We beat the spread!"

"What did you learn in school today that I'd object to?"

"This wasn't commissioned by the Emperor. This is just my random thoughts on stuff."

"I keep the good truth in the back."

"Oh, for goodness' sake—why don't you boys go out and shoot some hoops?"

INDEX OF ARTISTS